"If anyone knows how to hang art, it's Liz! Her curatorial eye is exquisite, and her approach to living with art is so warm and accessible. You don't need to be an expert in art to want special, beautiful, wonderful pieces in your home—and this book shows you how to do exactly that."

DANIELLE KRYSA author, artist, and founder of The Jealous Curator

"I have been with Liz since the early origins of her art career. We have worked beautifully together, and she has assisted many to become new collectors of art. I'm proud to be part of her journey, and this book is a testament to her knowledge and expertise in this field."

HUNT SLONEM artist

"*Art for Everyone* is a burst of encouragement for anyone who has ever hesitated to hang a piece of art. Liz Lidgett shows that art isn't about rules or prestige—it's about joy. With humor, clarity, and generosity, she makes the art world less intimidating and infinitely more fun. This is the art book we've been waiting for."

INGRID FETELL LEE author of *Joyful*

"*Art for Everyone* is a joyful guide that proves collecting art isn't just for experts or those with unlimited budgets—it's for all of us. Liz Lidgett breaks down barriers with clarity and warmth, offering practical tips that make art accessible, personal, and fun. This book will inspire you to see your walls as full of potential and possibility."

FARNOOSH TORABI host of the *So Money* podcast

"*Art for Everyone* is a refreshing guide that strips away the mystery and intimidation often surrounding art collecting. Liz Lidgett writes with the authority of an expert and the warmth of a trusted friend, offering readers both inspiration and practical tools to bring meaningful art into their lives."

OMA BLAISE FORD former senior executive editor for *Better Homes & Gardens*

ART for EVERYONE

Previous page: Artwork by Nate Nettleton. *This page:* Artwork by Kit Porter, Angela Chrusciaki Blehm, and Shannon Coppage.

ART for EVERYONE

How to Collect Art & Personalize Your Space on Any Budget

LIZ LIDGETT

SIMON ELEMENT

NEW YORK AMSTERDAM/ANTWERP LONDON TORONTO SYDNEY/MELBOURNE NEW DELHI

SIMON
ELEMENT

An Imprint of Simon & Schuster, LLC
1230 Avenue of the Americas
New York, NY 10020

First Simon Element hardcover edition April 2026

SIMON ELEMENT is a registered trademark of Simon & Schuster, LLC

Simon & Schuster strongly believes in freedom of expression and stands against censorship in all its forms. For more information, visit BooksBelong.com.

For information about special discounts for bulk purchases, please contact Simon & Schuster Special Sales at 1-866-506-1949 or business@simonandschuster.com.

The Simon & Schuster Speakers Bureau can bring authors to your live event. For more information or to book an event, contact the Simon & Schuster Speakers Bureau at 1-866-248-3049 or visit our website at www.simonspeakers.com.

Book cover and interior design by Laura Palese

All photography in this book by Adam Albright, unless otherwise noted.

Manufactured in China

1 3 5 7 9 10 8 6 4 2

Library of Congress Control Number: 2025938881

ISBN 978-1-6680-7870-9
ISBN 978-1-6680-7871-6 (ebook)

TO THE ARTISTS IN THIS BOOK: You make the world a more beautiful place. Thank you. Keep Going.

TO NICK, ROCKY, AND EFFIE: You make my world the most beautiful place. I love you.

Opposite: Background artwork by Christina Flowers. *This page:* Artwork by Michelle Armas.

This page: Artwork by Hillary Howorth, Keavy Murphree, Klein Reid, Beau Jones, and Rolando Rosler. Design by Gina Julian. Photo by Shannon Fontaine. *Opposite:* Background artwork by Christina Flowers.

Contents

INTRODUCTION

For more than ten thousand years, people have been decorating their homes with art. From caves to cabins, from huts to houses, art has been used to enliven and enrich spaces and to make people happy. The need to express ourselves through our décor unites humans across time. Blank walls are aching for portraits, barren stairways are begging for wallpaper, forlorn foyers are desperate for colors. If a home has at least four walls and a roof, that means there are no fewer than four opportunities in every building to showcase artwork (and even the roof is in play if you're creative). This book was created for those opportunities.

When I began my company more than a decade ago, it was my goal to become a crusader against blank walls. #nomoreblankwalls, I say. For too long, people have been made to feel that they don't belong in the art world or that there's a "right" way to collect art. About twice a week someone says to me, "Oh, I can't imagine what you would think of my home, I'd be so embarrassed." First, it's important that you know this: I am not here to judge you or your decorating style. Second, I've seen it all and I want to help! There are tips and tricks that you can master to take away any fear in decorating your walls. Remember: The goal is not to impress other people but to create a more joyful space for yourself.

I've become incredibly passionate over the years about eliminating the stigma and anxiety that surrounds buying and decorating with original artwork. You've heard of FOMO? Well, I believe too many people have FOLS—fear of looking stupid. It doesn't exactly roll off the tongue, but nevertheless, people have FOLS about walking into a gallery and feeling out of place. They fear speaking with an artist and asking the wrong questions, they fear buying the "wrong" piece, and they really fear putting the damn nail in the wall to hang a piece of artwork or hang a sheet of wallpaper. I've spoken with hundreds of clients who tell me they actually own artwork but have never hung it on the wall because they're worried if they do it, they'll do it wrong, and the wall will end up looking like Swiss cheese.

Artwork by Sydney Zester, Meghan Bustard, and Kathleen Jones.

CAPRI DOLCE VITA
TULUM
ASPEN

There are rules to follow that are easy to learn and will take your art fears away. Within the pages of this book, you'll find just how large a piece of artwork should be to go above your sofa or mantel. I'll teach you the exact right height at which to hang a picture, so you'll never have to argue with your spouse about it again. (My job often ends up being part art adviser, part marriage counselor.) You'll feel confident to play with pattern on your walls or pick a bold color.

OK, but who am I to teach you these things? I began my career as a corporate art adviser, and quickly my company evolved so that I was helping small businesses, restaurants, and people in their own homes. In 2019, I opened Liz Lidgett Gallery + Design to create a small but mighty art-world utopia. We have several guideposts that help us do business in a way that feels special to both our artists and our clients. For example, we maintain a rule that at least half the artists we represent are women. I was dismayed by the way female artists are underrepresented in both museums and galleries. I have seen reports that list female representation in galleries as low as just 13 percent. I felt that even though I may not be able to change the entire gallery world, I can make sure that I do it right—while representing the artists I find interesting. This is in addition to supporting BIPOC artists to make sure we give wall space, marketing dollars, and encouragement to all artists who are often overlooked.

This isn't a book for those who want to make money on the art market or "flip" a piece of artwork. It's for those of us who want to live with artwork we love. The majority of my clients spend anywhere from $100 to $5,000 on a piece of art. My clients are not millionaires, and they don't have a budget equal to the GDP of a small nation. They don't have master's degrees in art history. They're everyday people who enjoy art and want to have beautiful walls. I've said it time and time again: Art-collecting and decorating are about using your design eye, not your bank account. This book is for those of you who want to begin collecting artwork, not investing.

Opposite: Artwork by Taelor Fisher, Allison James, Kate Blomquist, and Betsy Enzensberger. Photo by Rick Lozier. Background artwork by Daisy Faith.

If you know where to look and what you're looking for, you can take down those posters from your college days and decorate with real, original artwork on any budget. My hope for you is to find the perfect piece of artwork for your style, space, and budget. I want to educate anyone and everyone, because living with original artwork is good for you. Supporting local and national artists is great for our economy and, most important, you deserve to love your home.

When you have a project at home looming over you, it can be stressful, especially if you don't know where to begin. In the following chapters, you'll have all the information at your fingertips to decorate your home with beautiful, original, affordable artwork. After you read this book, you'll know how to find your style, how to purchase a piece you love, how to frame it, and how to install it. I'll share some of my favorite projects, which are meant to inspire you and, quite frankly, you can copy the exact design if you're so inclined. The majority of the work used in this book was created by contemporary artists, meaning artists working today. So if you fall in love with a piece shown here, you can use these exact tips and find a piece by that very same artist. Finding the art that you love may literally be at your fingertips right now.

A homeowner is an artist with a canvas on every wall. At the end of this book, you'll have all the tools you need to fill your space with artwork and to find joy in the process.

Opposite: Artwork by Allison James.
Design by Massop House.

GABRIEL PRIZE
GREAT ART BY A GREAT ARTIST

This page: Artwork by Vicky Reddish and Taylor Cox; purse painted by Sarah Schwartz. *Opposite:* Background artwork by Christina Flowers.

CHAPTER

YOUR WALLS TELL A Story

ONE

WHY SHOULD YOU live with and collect ART?

Art in all its forms is a vital and essential part of society. For the purposes of this book, we will be focusing on visual art and how you can incorporate it into your life and home. Art has the ability to say what words cannot. It has the ability to calm or energize you, it can make you feel sorrow or find hope, or it can reveal the darkest parts of society and the most transcendent beauty in everyday life. It can help you look at both history and our contemporary world with new eyes and share new points of view. Art can help you look inside yourself to find new depths and insights or trigger memories to review in a new light.

Increasingly, doctors and psychologists are recognizing the therapeutic benefits of visiting museums and interacting with art. "Social prescribing" is the practice of recommending cultural activities to aid in the treatment of mental-health issues, loneliness, and even chronic conditions. Additionally, psychologists and therapists are using art therapy (visiting museums or making art) as part of a larger structured treatment plan for conditions like anxiety, depression, PTSD, and neurodegenerative diseases like dementia or Alzheimer's.

Beyond the mental-health benefits, your purchases and art engagement will stimulate the cultural economy on a more macro level and, on a micro level, you will support an artist and their dreams. With many purchases, you may find only a few days, months, or a couple of years of enjoyment out of them, but your art purchases can last a lifetime and create a legacy. Living in a home surrounded by beauty can help calm your nervous system and help you enjoy your everyday environment. Ultimately it can be summed up like this: Live with art, it's good for you.

YOUR WALLS TELL A STORY.

what story do you want

THEM TO TELL?

Each time I sit down with a new client, I ask the same questions. My hope is to get a snapshot of who they are and how they spend their time. I ask how they want to feel when they walk into the room, their likes and dislikes, where they like to vacation, and how they love to spend a Saturday afternoon. The answers to these questions come together to tell me a story about their aesthetic, their passions, and where they find joy. And it's this story that I ultimately want to help them tell through the art in their home. If you love to bike, it may be a piece that shows an actual bicycle, or I may find an artist who uses bicycle parts in an innovative way, or it may be an abstract piece that has a pattern that mimics a spoke or wheel. It may be literal, or it may not be. Ultimately, I want your walls to tell the story of you, the places you love to visit, the things you love to do—pieces of art that make you feel happy, that make you feel like you're home.

WHAT IS your "why"?

I encourage you to reflect on why you are interested in collecting art. Is it because of pure aesthetic considerations? Is it a way to express your personality? Your values? Do you want to support a specific artist or culture? Do you want to build a collection of family heirlooms? Do you want to create an emotional connection? We all have motivations when building a collection, and these motivations can help steer decisions and purchases when you are being thoughtful about them. Your "why" can be a powerful driving force in your collection and help to make some decisions easier.

HOW DO YOU FIND your style?

Once you're ready to begin collecting art, it's time to find your style. This can feel like a monumental task, but how do you eat an elephant? One bite at a time. If you take learning about art in small increments, then over time you will have learned a great deal about yourself and fine art. No one expects you to know everything about art, every artist, or every movement. Later on, we'll talk about information and terminology that will give you confidence in your conversations about art, but first, we need to just look. Being observant about the art (or lack of art) around you is your first mission. If you're aware and present when observing a room you're in, or when walking around an art gallery, or even as you're reading through a décor magazine, you'll begin to see what you respond to. Does the piece make you smile? Do you want to get closer? Do you want to spend time with it? If a work of art does any of

Artwork by Elisa Sheehan and AK Hardeman.

WHAT DO I SEE?

The artist Ron Giusti has created a modern botanical painting of an orchid. The piece is framed in a light wood that helps the artwork be the star of the show. What colors are used? Giusti has strong color contrasts, with crisp lines to the shapes so that color is a bold part of the artwork. The magenta, red, white, and green complement one another and create a minimalistic but powerful composition. What do I think about the artist's intention? Giusti is inspired by how simple shapes can say more than words. His goal was to be graphic and bold, and I believe he was successful.

these things for you—take note! Take a photograph, keep a note on your phone of artists' names and where you saw them. Keep a running list of things that catch your eye and revisit it when you're ready to buy or have a space in mind.

One very simple thing I do to get myself to slow down when viewing an artwork is to mentally ask myself questions about the work: What do I see? What colors do I see, and do those colors affect the mood or energy of the piece? How does this piece make me feel? Do I like it? Do I understand how it was made? Do I think that the artist is successful in what they were trying to achieve with this piece? I believe any piece of art has merit, even if it was just a way for the artist to express themself.

A breakdown like this for each work may seem simple or even tedious, but with practice, it will feel like second nature. Asking yourself questions about an artwork and what you are seeing is a powerful exercise to help you stay present in the moment and to slow down while looking at art. This can become a lovely meditation of sorts.

I also have a way I like to look at each piece. You may be thinking, Now she's even telling me how to *look* at a piece of art? But yes, yes, I am. I've read a number of studies, and on average, people look at an artwork for around fifteen seconds or less. In my experience, there are often artworks that reveal themselves over time. The longer I look, the more I see, and the more I like. So I do try to give each piece at least a full sixty seconds to make sure I have seen all I should. I start by approaching the piece head-on, from about ten feet back. I slowly walk up close to the piece. A joke in the art world is that you can always tell who is an artist by how close they get to an artwork. Artists always want to press their nose against the glass to see every brushstroke and each gesture and movement the artist made. Then I walk from one side to the other. If it's an unframed piece, the edges of the canvas can be incredibly revealing and interesting and give insight into the artist's process. For example, an edge can reveal the way paint drips dried, showing whether the artist turned the artwork multiple times while working on the piece. I know many artists who do not decide which side is the "top" of the piece until it is fully complete!

Opposite: Artwork by Ron Giusti.

LET'S TALK ABOUT THE

ANATOMY OF

When you are looking at an artwork, there is a checklist that you can mentally go through that will help you observe and learn more about a piece. I find this checklist most helpful if I am not responding well to a piece. Going through each element in my mind helps me break the artwork down and then see it again as the sum of its parts. Often the checklist has helped me notice something I hadn't seen before and find new appreciation in what the artist has created.

THE ELEMENTS OF A WORK OF ART

LINE: This element creates any shape or texture. Lines can create movement. As the artist Paul Klee said, "A line is a dot that went for a walk."

SHAPE: This element encloses areas using lines or color. Shapes can be geometric or organic. They can be representative of an object or abstract.

FORM: The 3-D effect created by lines, shape, and color.

COLOR: This element is the hue of the lines, shapes, and forms. Color also refers to the value, meaning lightness or darkness, and intensity.

VALUE: This element encompasses the use of light and dark, which create depth, contrast, and shadow.

TEXTURE: This is the surface quality or feeling. It can be tactile, such as a rough texture created in paint or stone, or implied, created through visual cues.

SPACE: This element arranges all of the above elements into a composition. Space can create depth, balance, and proportion.

AN ARTWORK

Once you understand these elements of art, you can begin thinking about how each of them are arranged in a work of art. This creates the principles of design. These are how designers and art historians analyze artwork or design. Next we'll look at how certain principles guide how all these elements interact and how they've evolved through the centuries through the contributions of artists, architects, and theorists.

THE PRINCIPLES OF DESIGN

BALANCE: This principle describes visual weight and how it is distributed throughout a piece. For example, is the piece symmetrical or asymmetrical with its elements?

CONTRAST: This principle describes the relationship between light versus dark, heavy versus light, big versus small, or rough versus smooth, to name a few.

EMPHASIS: This principle describes the focal point, or in other words, where your eye is drawn.

MOVEMENT: This principle defines the path the viewer's eye follows from element to element in the composition.

PATTERN: This principle is created through the repetition of elements.

PROPORTION AND SCALE: This is the relationship between elements in terms of their size.

UNITY AND VARIETY: This principle plays with the cohesiveness between elements while still creating visual interest.

If you run through these concepts in your head while you look at a piece, you'll be more thoughtful than 99 percent of the population looking at artwork. If studies say that an average person looks at a piece of artwork in a gallery or museum for fifteen seconds, anecdotally, as an observer in a gallery setting, I would say it's closer to ten seconds. This means that each time someone encounters an artwork, they are not only overlooking the formal design elements, but they may not even be truly looking at the piece. No one has time to review all of these elements each time they see a piece, but it's worth thinking about if you find a piece you're drawn to or feel negatively about. Here are three pieces I think are successful. I have broken down their elements and why they work.

This artwork by Andrea Ferrigno is a vibrant example of geometric abstraction. It utilizes bold colors and structured forms to create a visually dynamic composition. Let's analyze it using the elements of art as a framework:

Artwork by Andrea Ferrigno.

LINE: The painting is composed of clean, precise lines that define the geometric shapes. The curved and diagonal lines intersect, which add movement and guide the eye across the composition.

SHAPE: The piece features a combination of triangles, circles, and rectangles, emphasizing a structured composition. The balance between angular and curved shapes creates contrast and harmony.

COLOR: A vivid, warm palette of yellows, oranges, and reds is complemented by cool blues and purples.

TEXTURE: There is a smooth, even application of oil and acrylic paint, which creates a flat texture.

SPACE: The overlapping shapes and strategic placement of color creates a sense of depth and layering.

VALUE: Light and dark tones are used to create contrast and dimension.

FORM: The painting has been created on a canvas and is two-dimensional.

Andrea's abstract painting uses color, line, and shape to create a harmonious and visually balanced composition. It feels fluid and energetic.

This artwork by Paige Ledom is a collage-based still life that represents a realistic yet fragmented depiction of items found in a refrigerator. Using the elements of art as a framework again, let's analyze it!

Artwork by Paige Ledom.

LINE: The composition features a mix of sharp, angular lines and soft, curved edges that mimic the forms of various grocery items. The layering of paper cutouts creates implied lines, guiding the viewer's eye across the shelves.

SHAPE: The artwork is constructed using a variety of organic and geometric shapes. Rounded objects like lemons, jars, and bottles contrast with rectangular packaging and shelving to create visual balance.

COLOR: There is a diverse color palette represented in the food packaging. The colors are varied and create a representation of the chaotic nature of most fridge interiors.

TEXTURE: Since this is a collage, texture plays an important role. The layering of the paper and printed text from the paint swatches used as the medium provides a tactile quality. The texture of each fridge item is implied through the paper choices and cut lines.

SPACE: The shelves provide a structured, layered space and there is a sense of depth. The overlapping items and variation of size and detail enhance the perspective.

VALUE: The artist uses different shades of paper to create highlights and shadow, giving each object volume.

FORM: The work is two-dimensional but has some elements of cut paper that are not smooth, which creates a three-dimensional feel.

Paige's work is a masterful example of contemporary collage and realism, blending everyday objects with intricate detail and craftsmanship.

Finally, let's analyze the photographic work of artist Fares Micue. Her photograph presents a human figure curled into flowers, creating a surreal and emotionally evocative composition.

Artwork by Fares Micue.

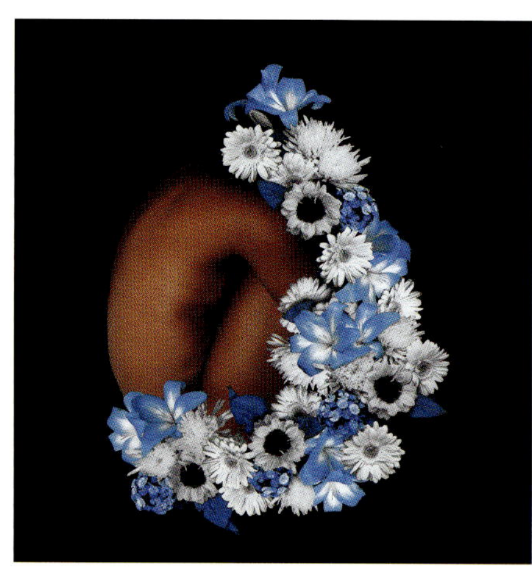

LINE: The curved posture of the figure forms a natural, flowing organic line, drawing attention to the shape and contours of the body. The flowers are arranged in a corresponding arc, creating circular movement for the central object.

SHAPE: The human body introduces soft, rounded shapes in comparison to the more structural floral elements. The florals also add depth and variation as each shape is layered.

COLOR: The palette is limited and powerful, with the black background forcing the body and florals to the foreground. The natural skin tone and blue, black, and white stand out and become more important because of the contrast.

TEXTURE: The smooth, almost velvety texture of the skin contrasts with the delicate texture of the flowers. The combination of realism with digital collage techniques adds further contrast between soft and crisp textures.

SPACE: The black background creates negative space, which isolates the subject.

VALUE: The interplay of light and shadow on the body and florals gives the entire composition a sculptural quality.

FORM: The figure appears three-dimensional although residing in a two-dimensional object like a framed photograph. The layering of flowers over the body enhances the illusion of volume and movement, as they seem to almost emerge from the figure.

This piece blends surrealism, portraiture, and digital collage techniques to explore themes of growth, transformation, and identity. The contrast of the body and flowers against the background invites the viewer to think about the symbolism behind the image, revealing a deeper narrative, perhaps one of rebirth, healing, or connection to nature.

Running through these compositional elements gives us a perfect framework to answer the question "What am I looking at?" You may not always be able to discern the medium or identify each material or grasp the meaning that the artist was trying to convey—90 percent of getting it "right" when talking about artwork is just *thinking* about the piece. Many artists will tell you that they feel their artwork is successful if it begins a conversation. It doesn't matter as much what you are saying about the piece, as long as it is making you think.

I feel so passionate about the idea that art is for everyone. Art can be purchased on any budget. And in this book, I want to help people build an art collection that is unique to them and only them. A collection that can't be re-created or purchased from a catalog. There are many ways to build an art collection—to impress your friends, to make investments, to match your room—but the only way I am interested in is building an art collection that you connect with. A collection that you love. When friends and family walk into your home, I want them to think, Ah, yes, this feels like my friend. I know more about them by seeing their home.

Try it. Go to your local museum with a friend and play a game where you pretend everything is for sale and money is no object. You and your friend each have to pick which artwork you would buy, and you must say *why*. Articulating what you like about a piece is an important part of buying art and the learning experience. Bonus points if you say where you'd put the artwork in your home.

DO I HAVE TO LIKE EVERY PIECE OF ART? WHAT IF

I just don't get it?

The short answer is no, of course not! The long answer is a bit more nuanced. As a gallery owner, I see a lot of artwork while I am looking for artists to represent or finding new work for my clients. The truth, which may sound cruel at first, is that I am not drawn to most artwork. That's what's exciting about the work I truly do love. Even when I don't prefer a piece, I still see its value. Value, in this case, means that it was important for the artist to create it, and it will mean something to its owner. Artwork was created equally—all are worthy. As you look at more art over time, most likely you will become more discerning about what you are drawn to.

I try to refrain from using words like "good" or "bad." I focus more on a conversation about whether the artwork is successful. Artwork is subjective, and what is unsuccessful for me may be incredibly successful for another viewer. Focusing on success also leads to the conversation of understanding the artist's intent.

One last note on intent: I was taught in college that an artist's intent is what makes an object a work of art. You may have heard someone sometime exclaim, "That's not art!" when judging something they don't like or think is too simplistic, or any number of reasons people dismiss pieces. Well, I don't believe it's up to the viewer to decide what is art and what's not. If an artist created or installed an object as a work of art, then it is in fact an artwork. This mindset really helps to end a lot of silly art arguments and leads to a more inclusive conversation in the art world.

If you come across a piece you view as unsuccessful while you are in search of an artwork for your home, I recommend acting like the artist is in the room (and sometimes they may be). A simple "I don't prefer it" or "That's not my favorite" would suffice. As you become more discerning on the topic of art, it is helpful to voice your opinion in a thoughtful and polite way to an artist or a gallerist if they are helping you search for a piece. It may be that you don't love a certain color, size, texture, or compositional element. These notes become very helpful when helping you find the perfect piece.

Artwork by
Nate Nettleton.

Artwork *(above)* by: Laura Palmer, Ron Giusti, Chris Vance, Van Holmgren, Makiko Harris, and Chad Wys. Background artwork by Christina Flowers.

But please, promise me right now, you will never say, "My kid could do that." Truly, unless your kid is Matisse, they could not. Even more important, they didn't. I know I don't have to worry about that with you, though; we can be critically kind in our conversations about art.

HOW DO YOU CREATE A meaningful collection?

My main goal is for you to buy art that you love and that has special meaning for you—not art that matches your couch. My favorite art collections are the ones that tell me more about a person, collections that are diverse and don't necessarily "match" but seem to flow because they tell the story of a beautiful life. The invisible string that connects the collection is the collector.

There are so many ways to start a collection. One client of mine even helps their children start their art collections at age thirteen. Each following year, the child is given an artwork for their birthday so that by the time they are ready for a place of their own, they have art for their walls. Most of my clients begin collecting one piece at a time, slowly building as their budget and space allow. Somewhere along the line the media has convinced us that good paintings only sell for millions of dollars. Sure, there are museum-worthy artworks that do command those figures, but there is a large and beautiful art world out there that is accessible.

Whether your parents helped you start your collection as a child or you're starting it on your own, it's never too early or too late to begin. Right now seems like the perfect time to me, in fact. Here are three ways I love to tell clients to create a meaningful collection.

1. Buy art as your souvenir when you travel.

In my mind, the very best way to remember the time you were running up the Spanish Steps in Rome, or when you came across a charming town on a road trip through New England, is by buying a piece of art as a souvenir. I place a small amount of money in my travel budget for each trip. The piece of art that hangs above my bed is a piece I paid $35 for at a *brocante* (flea market) on a special trip to Strasbourg, France. It has a small tear in the weathered canvas, and the frame has corners chipped away, but none of that matters because of my memories of walking through the stalls and enjoying that quintessential French experience. Price, age, even condition don't need to have anything to do with how special a piece is or what it means to you. I adore the antique painting and its nowhere-near-perfect condition because it reminds me of that trip and makes me smile.

2. Get to know the artist.

Slowly but surely, I am collecting a piece from each artist whose work we carry in my gallery. I am so drawn to each piece aesthetically, but it means even more because I know the artist personally and have a story about each person and piece. Of course, you don't have to own a gallery to follow this tip. Your local art festival or maker's market is a great place to shop for art while getting to know the artist. It is often the case that the artists themselves are staffing their own booths or tables and feel honored to talk about their work.

3. Buy a piece of artwork to celebrate milestones.

My friend, artist Angela Chrusciaki Blehm, sent me a piece of artwork to honor the birth of my daughter, Effie. It's hung proudly in Effie's room, and each time I see it I think of Angela and those wonderful but foggy days with a newborn and the surprise of receiving it. It also started Effie's own art collection. Marking milestones like birthdays, anniversaries, or an event you're proud of, like a promotion, is a wonderful reason to buy a piece of art.

In the past I have also advised collectors to create a "theme" or a running narrative to their collection. These themes can help narrow a focus and put parameters around the collection. For example, I work with a female-owned law office, and we have helped them create a collection that focuses on female artists. It reinforces what is special about their law firm while also supporting artists who are inspiring to them. If a particular point of view or experience is important to you, then I urge you to support artists who represent those ideas.

Another client I have worked with for many years began collecting when she and her husband were newly married. They focused on purchasing pieces that featured "twos," whether in objects, canvases, or somewhere in the design to represent them as a couple. As their family began to grow, they collected pieces that included threes and then fours. Their collection represents their family story throughout their home. It's subtle while being personally meaningful.

A theme is not a necessity, because *you* the collector are the invisible string that connects each piece to the next. You may even think of your artwork in the sense of "mini collections" within one larger collection. I have a client, for example, who loves to buy portraits of people she doesn't know. She has them in a large gallery wall going up her stairs. She keeps this mini collection together in one location, and throughout her home are the other wonderful, eclectic pieces she owns.

If you buy what you love, you may find that retrospectively there are clear themes to be found in the pieces you own. Most important, though, buying what you love will ensure you'll never regret your decision.

This page: Artwork is a collection of vintage paintings with work by Janet Hill Studio. Design by Elsie Larson. Photo by Katie Day. *Opposite:* Background artwork by Daisy Faith.

CHAT LIKE AN EXPERT

Do you feel nervous about starting a conversation with an artist? Here are a couple of conversation starters that will help you feel more at ease. The most important thing to know is that artists are often very excited to talk about their work with interested clients. Being an artist can be a solitary experience unless they have worked to intentionally create community. Speaking with an artist gives them much-needed feedback and insight into their clients and potential clients while also informing you about the artwork. It's a win-win!

"I love your work! Please tell me more about your process."

"You are so talented. How did you get started?"

"I am so drawn to this piece. Can you tell me about the inspiration?"

These conversations and the tidbits you learn will help create meaning and a story for each work of art. The more you talk with artists and talk about art, the easier it will become.

WHAT ARE THE MOST common types OF ARTWORK?

There are many different types of artwork that you may potentially buy throughout your lifetime. Below are the most common that you will interact with.

1. Painting

OIL PAINTING: Rich, vibrant, and slow-drying for blending (think Van Gogh, Rembrandt).

ACRYLIC PAINTING: Fast-drying and versatile, often used in modern art.

WATERCOLOR PAINTING: Light and fluid, often used for landscapes and portraits.

MIXED MEDIA: Combines different paints or materials for texture and depth.

2. Drawing

PENCIL DRAWING: Great for sketches, realism, and shading techniques.

CHARCOAL DRAWING: Deep contrast, often used for dramatic effects.

INK OR PEN DRAWING: Used for fine details, line art, and illustration.

3. Sculpture

BRONZE SCULPTURE: A classic medium for statues and historical figures.

MARBLE OR STONE SCULPTURE: Often used in classical and religious works.

WOOD OR CLAY SCULPTURE: Used for intricate carvings or contemporary pieces.

4. Printmaking

ETCHING AND ENGRAVING: Creates detailed prints using metal plates.

WOODBLOCK AND LINOCUT: A relief print method where the design is carved out.

SCREEN PRINTING: Popular in commercial and pop art (think Andy Warhol).

5. Photography

FINE ART PHOTOGRAPHY: Expressive and artistic rather than documentary.

BLACK-AND-WHITE PHOTOGRAPHY: Timeless and moody compositions.

STREET OR DOCUMENTARY PHOTOGRAPHY: Captures real-life moments.

Artwork by Angie Heuton.

6. Digital Art

ILLUSTRATION AND CONCEPT ART: Used in media, gaming, and book covers.

3-D MODELING AND CGI: Creates virtual sculptures and digital worlds.

NFTS AND CRYPTO ART: Digital art that exists on blockchain platforms.

7. Textile and Fiber Art

TAPESTRY AND WEAVING: Fabric-based art, often intricate and decorative.

EMBROIDERY AND QUILTING: Uses thread and stitching to create detailed images.

8. Collage and Assemblage

COLLAGE: Uses cutout images, paper, and textures for layered artwork.

ASSEMBLAGE: 3-D collage using found objects and materials.

9. Installation Art

Large-scale, immersive works that transform spaces, often interactive.

Opposite: Artwork by Angie Heuton. *This page:* Artwork by Marcy Cook Vreeland, Joy Kinna, Aly Ytterberg, Logan Ledford, and vintage pieces.

CAN YOU TELL ME MORE ABOUT DIFFERENT

art styles?

Humans have been creating art for more than forty thousand years. In the entirety of art history, there are countless specific styles, each one building off the next. Styles go in and out of fashion, influencing each next generation of artists. So how can I boil it down to a proper overview when the topic can, and does, fill countless books? I have listed below the most common contemporary styles that you will most often have to reference. My recommendation to you is to dive into a brief education about each style. As I was going through the "elements of art" exercise for you, we already mentioned some of these styles, but I'd like to give you the proper foundation as you are looking for art to begin your collection. I am also going to give you a piece to search online that will be representative of the style. Many of these works will be masterpieces or iconic to our society in some way. You may even be able to just think of the piece rather than having to run to Google, because they are that well known.

REALISM: This is a detailed and lifelike re-creation of subjects that can range from still lifes to portraits to landscapes and beyond. "Representational" is also often referenced in relation to realism.

A famous piece in this style: *The Gleaners* by Jean-François Millet, created in 1857. Can be seen in person at the Musée d'Orsay in Paris.

IMPRESSIONISM: This style is known by the visible brushstrokes created by an artist and the emphasis on light and movement. Impressionism is characterized by often capturing ephemeral or fleeting moments. The style has its roots in artists sharing everyday life and the things the artists saw, experienced, and felt.

A famous piece in this style: *Impression, Sunrise* by Claude Monet, created in 1872. Can be seen in person at the Musée Marmottan Monet in Paris.

ABSTRACTION: This style is the counter to realism through nonrepresentational art. These pieces focus on form, color, and shape and express thoughts and feelings through those elements rather than realistic depictions. You may also see, from time to time, abstract work that is based in reality such as "floral abstraction" or "figural abstraction."

A famous piece in this style: *Composition VII* by Wassily Kandinsky, created in 1913. Can be seen in person at the State Tretyakov Gallery in Moscow.

SURREALISM: These artworks are often dreamlike, with otherworldly compositions. Surrealism often verges into the bizarre or "weird" and the subconscious mind. This style is realism gone awry.

A famous piece in this style: *The Persistence of Memory* by Salvador Dalí, created in 1931. Can be seen in person at the Museum of Modern Art in New York.

EXPRESSIONISM: Think intense, emotive artworks that focus on color and form to share what the artist is feeling. Often is based in abstraction (Abstract Expressionism, for example), and can include gestural styles. This means you can almost picture the artist painting, splashing, or dripping their paint (or any other medium) onto the canvas.

A famous piece in this style: *The Scream* by Edvard Munch, created in 1893. Can be seen in person at the National Museum in Oslo.

A famous piece in Abstract Expressionism: *Autumn Rhythm (Number 30)* by Jackson Pollock, created in 1950. Can be seen at the Metropolitan Museum of Art in New York.

CUBISM: Pablo Picasso is the father of Cubism. He developed a style that breaks down objects into geometric shapes and multiple perspectives. This means that a person's face, for example, shows all angles in a flat plane across the canvas.

A famous piece in this style: *Les Demoiselles d'Avignon* by Pablo Picasso, created in 1907. Can be seen in person at the Museum of Modern Art in New York.

MINIMALISM: This style uses simple shape, color, line, and space to create a very clean aesthetic. Restraint and pared-down color palettes are the stars for artists creating minimalistic works.

A famous piece in this style: *With My Back to the World* by Agnes Martin, created in 1997. Can be seen in person at the Museum of Modern Art in New York.

POP ART: A sense of fun, energy, references to popular culture, as well as bold use of color are all important hallmarks of pop art. You'll often see commercial images and mass-production techniques used throughout the works.

A famous piece in this style: *Marilyn Diptych* by Andy Warhol, created in 1962. Can be seen in person at the Tate Modern in London.

ART DECO: The early twentieth century created this glamorous and geometric-based style. It influenced so many things in culture at the time—architecture, fashion, and the visual arts.

A famous piece in this style: *The Kiss* by Gustav Klimt, created in 1908. Can be seen in person at the Österreichische Galerie Belvedere (the Austrian Gallery) in Vienna.

STREET ART: Not just limited to the streets, yet called "street art" or "graffiti," this is a bold and expressive style. Artists who create street art often make pieces based on politics and popular culture, and it thrives in public spaces.

A famous piece in this style: *Girl With Balloon* by Banksy, created in 2002. Can be seen in person in multiple locations, but the original mural is on the Waterloo Bridge in South Bank, London.

HOW DO I

commission artwork?

Commissioning artwork means that a client gets to work with an artist (or the gallery representing them) to create a new piece of artwork. Commissions are great options if you love the work or style of an artist but would like something created just for you, with consideration for specifics like size, color, or subject matter. Each artist I work with has a different level of comfort with the level of direction they'll take from a client. Many artists handle commission pricing differently. Some artists keep their size and pricing the same as their other works. Other artists include a small upcharge for a commission because it can be additional work for the artist. I cannot speak for every artist, but many I have worked with find commissions to be rewarding and a wonderful partnership between client and artist. Other artists do not prefer to work with the requests of a client. It is OK to ask an artist, respectfully, if they would be open to a commission. Sharing that you love an artist's work is always a compliment. A great approach would be "I am a big fan of your work. I love the way you use color and texture. I have looked through your current available works and need a piece a certain size. Would you be willing to work on a commission for me?"

HERE'S WHAT YOU SHOULD KNOW ABOUT

commissioning an artwork

Who's a good candidate?

The best type of client for a commissioned artwork is one who will give low levels of direction and let the artist do their thing. You love their work for a reason, so trust them to do it! An example I think back to is of a family that loved an artwork that had previously been sold. We asked the artist to create a new piece with the same subject matter (but not an exact copy), and we also knew that bees were quite special to the family. The artist created a new piece that incorporated a small, almost-hidden bee into the scene. Forever, the family will know that that piece was created just for them.

ART ETIQUETTE! Christoph Niemann, an illustrator and artist, is quoted as saying, "If you want to break an artist's heart, pay him/her a compliment that starts with 'Your work reminds me of . . .'" It's kind when speaking to an artist to focus on the things that you like about their work and not focus on what you have seen and liked from others. We would never want to ask an artist to copy another artist's style.

If you are commissioning a piece of artwork, please never ask an artist to create an exact copy of a previous work. An important part of original artwork is that each is unique. Additionally, an exact copy is never truly possible. Brushstrokes are as varied as fingerprints.

How are commissions priced?

Each artist works differently. Many artists price their work per square inch. Then for commissions, some artists may have a price increase of around 10 to 15 percent, because of the additional work involved. The extra time comes from discussions with the client and the approval of the final design. If a client does not like a particular element, then even more time can be spent reworking the composition. Some artists keep their pricing consistent regardless of whether it is a commission. It's a good idea to ask the artist or gallery about a price difference for commissions so you can factor that into your budget. Some artists also may have a price minimum for their commissions. It is also customary to pay 50 percent up front for the commission to begin. This acts as a deposit for materials and the artist's initial design time.

What are the benefits?

The benefits of a commissioned artwork are that you will end up with a piece that will work beautifully for you and your space. Again, each artist is different, but many will ask for your approval at one or two points throughout the process. They may have you approve a color palette they have created to get started or share a progress photo partway through the creation. My only cautionary note is to reiterate that you should allow the artist to do their "thing." We have had clients be genuinely thrilled about the commission process but become overly prescriptive about what they wanted in their artwork to the point where it took the creativity out of the process for the artist and the client was ultimately not satisfied. The goal is to find a happy medium where the artist can create freely while also making a piece that works for the client. When the process for a commission goes smoothly, there are really wonderful results. In my experience, artists often love when their galleries help with the commissions because we can handle some of the up-front conversations that will help the artists work with freedom.

If you'd like to commission an artwork, you can work with a gallery or directly with an artist. Here's a script for success:

Opposite: Background artwork by Daisy Faith.

SCRIPT FOR SUCCESS

Dear [artist],

I love your style and found your work [insert way in which you appreciate their work here]. I have done some research, and I'd love to work with you on a commission. Here's the information:

I'd like the following size: (h X w inches)

Attached is a photo of the space.

Attached are three screenshots of your work that speak to me.

If you have any specific requests (for example, color or subject matter that the artist often uses), now's the time to say!

Can you please confirm your availability? And if so, please confirm the pricing and timeline. Thank you for bringing so much beauty into the world!

Best,
Client

AN ARTFUL CONVERSATION WITH

SHERRY PETERSIK

OF YOUNG HOUSE LOVE

John and Sherry Petersik have fixed up seven homes, written two New York Times*–bestselling books, and have designed products sold in Target and Home Depot. On their site, YoungHouseLove.com, you'll find more than three thousand DIY projects and updates, including how they downsized to a 1,400-square-foot house.*

Artwork by June Street Studio and Michelle Armas. Photo and design by Sherry Petersik, Young House Love.

LIZ: **You have documented the process of downsizing into your dream home. How do you like to incorporate art in your smaller space to still have great style?**

SHERRY: In a smaller home, some large-scale art can really make the room! Just like my advice is not to fill a small space with lots of tiny furniture (so cluttered; larger pieces help the room feel expansive, so you can live large) . . . I give the same advice for art! Go big or go home. We did white walls here, so our little six-room beach house feels airier and open—and it's also the perfect backdrop for some large-scale art with color and texture that adds so much to each room.

LIZ: **What do you think about as you bring a new piece into your collection? Do you hope they all "go together," or do you just buy what you love?**

SHERRY: I tend to just buy what I love, but I do notice that I'm almost always drawn to things that end up "going together," so . . . trust those instincts! I find I always love soft pieces with lots of texture that can slip in anywhere, because they add so much depth and interest to a space. I also love bold abstracts and figural pieces, almost all of which have pinks, blues, greens, tans, and soft yellows. It's wild how similar palettes can grab you and look so good together throughout a home—even if they're entirely different styles, subjects, and sizes.

LIZ: **What's your favorite piece of artwork that you own and why?**

SHERRY: I have a snake by Paige Barnes Dorsey, and it's my pride and joy. It looks like a blue-and-white porcelain sculpture on the wall, and it's so interesting and fun that nearly everyone who comes over asks where they can get one. It's my "I'd save that in a fire for sure" art piece, but I'd try to grab, like, ten other things on the way out too. Collecting art that you love with every bone in your body is addicting. Don't say I didn't warn ya!

KINFOLK ISLANDS
AMALFI

A BRIEF

Glossary

OF TERMS

These are terms I want you to feel comfortable with when purchasing a piece of art. These words and definitions come up often when discussing artwork and are the jargon of the art world. I had a professor in grad school who would use huge (and, I argued, made-up) words while discussing art. I had a running document named "That Is Not a Real Word" that I would refer back to and look up later. I was right about half the time. Some people use language to make the art world intimidating or exclusive, and while that is a shame, most of these terms help people articulate how a piece makes them feel and what it means to them. My point is, there's a lot of terms that people in the art world use, perhaps unnecessarily, but if you know these, you'll do just fine.

This is not a traditional dictionary of terms. Below, I use my own words to describe concepts in a way that I hope is approachable and not just peppering you with more things you need to go look up.

Opposite: Artwork by Emily Keating Snyder. Design by Saltbox Design Co, Lauren Winter. Photo by Rae Scott.

Common Terms Used When Purchasing Artwork

APPRAISAL
A professional assessment of an artwork's value. This is often used for insurance or resale. Usually, an appraisal is not needed when purchasing from a gallery or artist in the primary market (defined below).

ARCHIVAL
Materials designed for long-term preservation, which will aid in preventing deterioration.

ARTIST'S PROOF
This is signified by the letters *AP* or *EA* (*épreuve d'artiste* in French). An AP is a special subset of a limited-edition print that is set aside for the artist's personal use. Traditionally, these were used for the artist to review the quality of the print before the final edition was produced.

BUYER'S PREMIUM
An additional fee charged by auction houses, typically a percentage of the sale price. This can be considered a "hidden cost" and is important to check before bidding.

CERTIFICATE OF AUTHENTICITY
Otherwise known as a CoA. This is a document that attests an artwork is authentic. Some artists provide these, other times galleries can provide them. Each artwork does not automatically have a CoA, but you can ask for one if that is important for you and your records. It typically includes the artwork's purchase price, date created, dimensions, medium, and often an artist's biography.

COMMISSION
An artwork created custom for a client by an artist upon request.

CONSIGNMENT
An arrangement where an artist or collector leaves artwork with a gallery to sell on their behalf.

DIPTYCH/TRIPTYCH/POLYPTYCH
These are artworks that consist of more than one piece. A diptych contains two pieces or panels, a triptych three, and a polyptych four or more.

EDITION
This describes works where there are more than one. It is often used for prints that have an open edition, meaning they will continue to print them on demand in perpetuity, or a limited edition, meaning they will cap the number of reproductions made.

FAIR MARKET VALUE
The estimated value of an artwork based on past sales and demand.

INHERENT VICE
This is a term used to describe artwork made from mediums that may change, crumble, rot, or even evaporate. Often used when referring to ephemeral, or non-permanent, materials.

MEDIUM
This describes the way that an artwork was made and what materials were used. This is a common identification that is used on both museum and gallery labels, along with artist, title, and date created.

ORIGINAL
This is a work of art that has no exact copies. However, it can be the basis for reproductions. For example, *Mona Lisa* is an original work of art that has many reproductions, on everything from posters to throw pillows.

PRICELIST
This is a document that a gallery can give you upon request that contains a list of retail prices for multiple works of art.

PRIMARY MARKET
This term refers to when an artwork is brought to market, or, in other words, comes up for sale for the first time at a gallery, an exhibition, or directly from the artist.

PROVENANCE
This is the history of an artwork. A strong provenance would show when an artwork is created and then where it has been located and how it was transferred (donation, sale, and so on) from owner to owner. This information is used for appraisals and auctions and sales on the secondary market.

RESALE RIGHTS (DROIT DE SUITE)
A royalty an artist may receive when their artwork is resold. This is important to understand for the secondary market (defined below).

RETAIL PRICE
The set price for an artwork by an artist or a gallery.

SECONDARY MARKET
This term refers to when an artwork reappears on the market after having been previously sold. The secondary market can include galleries that will sell works for clients (as opposed to selling them directly from an artist) and auctions. No matter how many times the artwork has been sold, it is still considered to be the secondary market.

TEAR SHEET
This is a document that shows a photo and information about the artwork including artist, title, dimensions, date created, medium, and sale price. This can be provided by a gallery for a client's reference.

Common Mediums

ACRYLIC PAINT
This is a type of paint that is made from synthetic acrylic resins. Acrylic is a very common type of paint used in artwork because of its buildable nature and the quick speed at which it dries.

CHALK
Similar to, but more high-quality than, the chalk you used as a child. Often used in sketching or preliminary drawings because chalk can easily be wiped away. The pigment and quality of the chalk can make the drawing more permanent.

CHARCOAL
These are charred sticks of wood used similarly to chalk, to create either sketches or permanent/finished drawings.

DIGITAL
This is artwork created using a computer or other digital device. As things progress, Artificial Intelligence (AI) can also help to create the work.

ENCAUSTIC
Often used with paintings or ceramics, it is a technique that uses hot wax and pigments mixed together to create an inlay that is burned into a surface.

GICLEE (PRONOUNCED ZHEE-CLAY)
This is a French term referring to a type of print created using a high-quality inkjet printer. Could be a part of an open or limited edition.

GLASS
Artworks made primarily of glass usually have no utilitarian function other than to be decorative.

GOUACHE
This is a material similar to watercolor and is opaque. While watercolors are often created by adding water to a compressed dry pigment, gouache is most often found in a paint tube and is created by combining a paint pigment and a binding agent that makes it liquid.

GRAPHITE
Works in graphite usually are made with a pencil, but graphite can be used in other forms and creates marks in that similar metallic-gray coloring.

INK
A pen is most commonly used to apply ink to a surface. An artist could also spill, dip, or paint with ink. Also often known as a pen drawing.

LITHOGRAPH
Lithography is a printmaking process where a design is drawn onto a flat stone or metal plate and affixed to a paper by a chemical reaction. Many lithographs use multiple plates and are most often black ink on white paper. Chromolithography refers to a print that is multicolor.

MIXED MEDIA
This is a term used to describe an artwork that uses multiple mediums, for example, painting and sewing on one surface like a canvas. Sometimes an artwork label may just read "mixed media," and other times it will list each medium used.

OIL PAINT
This is a type of paint that mixes pigment and drying oil as a binder. It has been one of the most common types of paints used for artwork for centuries. Acrylic is a newer type of paint developed in the 1930s, but oil paint dates back to at least the seventh century. It has a much longer drying time, which many artists prefer because you can manipulate the paint over the course of days.

PASTEL
The term "pastel" can refer to either a pencil or crayon-like instrument. Most commonly, it refers to pigments that have been ground and then rolled together into sticks using binding agents.

PHOTOGRAPHY
Photography literally means "drawing with light," derived from the Greek words for light and drawing, which is such a lovely concept. Photographs can be made using light-sensitive film or can be produced digitally. Photography most often comes from using a stand-alone camera but also can be created with devices that have cameras attached.

PRINTMAKING
This is the overarching term for many processes that are based on transferring an image from one surface to another. Most often an image is placed onto paper or fabric. There are many, many types of printmaking, but some to familiarize yourself with would be woodcutting, etching, engraving, lithography, and digital.

SCULPTURE
This is the art of making a 3-D object that can be either representational or abstract. Sculpture is often made from stone, wood, metal, plaster, or resin.

TEMPERA PAINT
Color pigments are most commonly combined with egg yolk to create this type of paint. It has been around for centuries and was once more popular than oils.

WATERCOLOR PAINT
Already compared above to gouache, this is a pigment that has been most often dried and compressed into a small block that then can be activated with a wet paintbrush. One of the main advantages of using watercolors is how an artist can build the pigment with multiple layers as they allow each layer to dry on a piece of paper.

As an aside, "inherent vice" is one of my favorite terms and definitions. It refers to a medium of work that may be unstable. There are examples where an artist has knowingly used a medium that will deteriorate or change over time. Those periods of times may vary, depending on the material used. For example, in 2019 an Italian artist, Maurizio Cattelan, created a work called *Comedian*. There was an edition of three and two artist proofs. It is a work of conceptual art made of a fresh banana affixed to a wall with duct tape. Since it is a piece of conceptual art, and the banana will rot quite quickly, what the artwork owner actually "owns" is the concept made of detailed diagrams and instructions for proper display, along with the certificate of authenticity. The inherent vice of the medium (a banana) is that the artist knows it will rot. I hesitate to tell you that each edition originally sold for $120,000 and then an edition sold in 2024 for $6.2 million at auction. *Comedian* has become a symbolic piece for how out of touch and bizarre the art world can be. This is the type of artwork that often makes the news, thereby making people feel they never will "get" art. I bring it up here because a banana is the perfect example of inherent vice. Other famous examples include Anselm Kiefer works that use mud throughout (the mud will crumble slowly but surely over the years); Eva Hesse's sculptures made of latex (the latex deteriorates quite quickly and becomes brittle); and Zoe Leonard's *Strange Fruit*, which consisted of fruit skins sewn back together after the fruit was consumed.

Back to our regularly scheduled programming! Here are some examples of artwork I have sold in my gallery, where I can display many of the terms just defined. Let's break them down with some of the concepts we just learned. The following are three examples of different artists who have created floral paintings. I am constantly in awe of how artists are able to take a directive like "please make a painting of flowers" and create such vastly different works of art. First up, we have three examples of representational artwork.

Opposite: Artwork by Kevin Brent Morris. Photo by Rick Lozier.

SIXTINE DUBLY
FLOWE

2

1

3

REPRESENTATIONAL ARTWORK

1. Here we have a painting, *Tapestry II,* by artist Brittany Smith. Her work is impressionistic, with loose brushstrokes, while being expressive and capturing the essence of the flowers rather than photorealistic details. Her work is mixed media for a layered technique on handmade cotton paper. With the flowers, known as Wild Quaker Ladies, not being rigidly defined, the viewer's eye is able to fill in the gaps and create a detailed image in their own mind. The grassy background in brushy shades of green is implied rather than directly represented. The composition is light and airy while using a palette of neutrals. This is a piece that would go beautifully with interiors that embrace a natural, soft aesthetic.

2. Next, we have an artwork, *Ruby*, by Michele Aschenbrenner. This work is a contemporary, abstract floral design based on bold, simplified shapes. The flowers and leaves are reduced to flat, organic forms without intricate details. As with Smith's work discussed above, Aschenbrenner invites the viewer to bring their own experiences into a piece and recall beautiful florals they have seen themself. Aschenbrenner's approach creates a modern and playful aesthetic with a bit of nostalgia, playing on midcentury graphic design. The color palette is warm, with corals and pinks, and balanced well with the cooler tones of blue and green. Without shading or texture, the shapes become all about the graphic quality and its pop-art influence shines through. The clean, hard edges look almost printed, but they are hand-painted with acrylic on board, finished with a varnish to the work.

3. Finally, we have the work of Nay Bellamy. This artwork presents a botanical realism style with a contemporary twist. In the foreground, there is the almost textbook-realistic illustration depicting flowers and leaves with great attention to detail. There is an emphasis on the organic texture and natural imperfection. There is also beautiful rendering of shadow and light to make the botanicals feel real, like they could almost curl up from the artwork. The foreground contrasts with the background, which offers a modern tonal striped pattern. The hard edges are the perfect contrast to the organic forms of the flowers and leaves. The palette, painted with acrylics and oils, is soft and earthy, being influenced by natural colors in warm yellows and deep greens. While the foreground and background contrast, the palette creates harmony with the muted colors.

These are three very different versions of floral painting, but none of them are a straightforward exact re-creation of a bouquet in a vase. Each showcases just one of endless possibilities that artists can create from a traditional, classic subject matter like flowers. It's important to understand some of the definitions, mediums, and styles written about in this chapter because it will help you speak about your likes and dislikes when looking for a work to purchase.

Opposite: Artwork by Brittany Smith (1), Michele Aschenbrenner (2), and Nay Bellamy (3).

Another common style you will see is abstract painting. "Abstract" almost feels like too general a term, meaning a style of painting where the artist does not attempt to directly represent reality but instead uses shapes, color, texture, and strokes to create a feeling or effect. But there are so many different forms of this style. Here are three pieces of art we can dissect.

ABSTRACT PAINTING

1. First, we have *First Day of Spring*, by Vicky Reddish, which showcases abstract expressionism with a gestural style. The repeated short, curved strokes and dashes create a sense of energy and fluidity. Each stroke is layered, and the overlapping colors add depth and complexity to give the painting a lively, organic feel. Abstract expressionism emphasizes emotion, spontaneity, and the physical act of painting. Often when I am seeing a painting for the first time, I like to close my eyes and picture the artist actually painting the piece, and I think you can feel Vicky's energy here. There is color harmony with an overall palette of blues and greens with complementary contrasting colors with the blush and coral. Most important, the piece is non-representational but does create the feeling of pattern without being exact.

2. Next, we have the work of Logan Ledford. This style is modern, abstract, and minimalist. The negative white space in the piece highlights the "quad-dots," which create a repetitive shape using a variety of colors. Each section showcases distinct color combinations that interact well and create a color-field aesthetic. The medium, acrylic paint, becomes just as important as what the paint depicts because of the thick, sculptural quality that it creates. Each piece is left to dry fully for weeks so that the peaks and valleys created with the paint can remain solid and intact. This is a work where you can study color relationships, balance, and minimalism.

3. Finally, we have *New Love Landscape* by artist Neicy Frey, which can be categorized as "biomorphic abstraction," which includes organic, fluid shapes. The forms feel natural and familiar yet ambiguous so that the style still fits squarely within the definition of "abstract." The soft, curvilinear shapes resemble natural elements like leaves, stones, florals, or coral and flow into one another. There is a muted and complementary color palette. The subdued blues, greens, grays, and earth tones create a balanced and dynamic visual effect for the viewer. Without shading or light variances the shapes are flat, creating color fields with soft edges. The use of oil paints on canvas feels timeless, with influences from midcentury modern art and design.

Again, we have seen three paintings that fit into one category of abstraction while still showing the variations and opportunities that can be created by artists.

Opposite: Artwork by Vicky Reddish (1), Logan Ledford (2), and Neicy Frey (3).

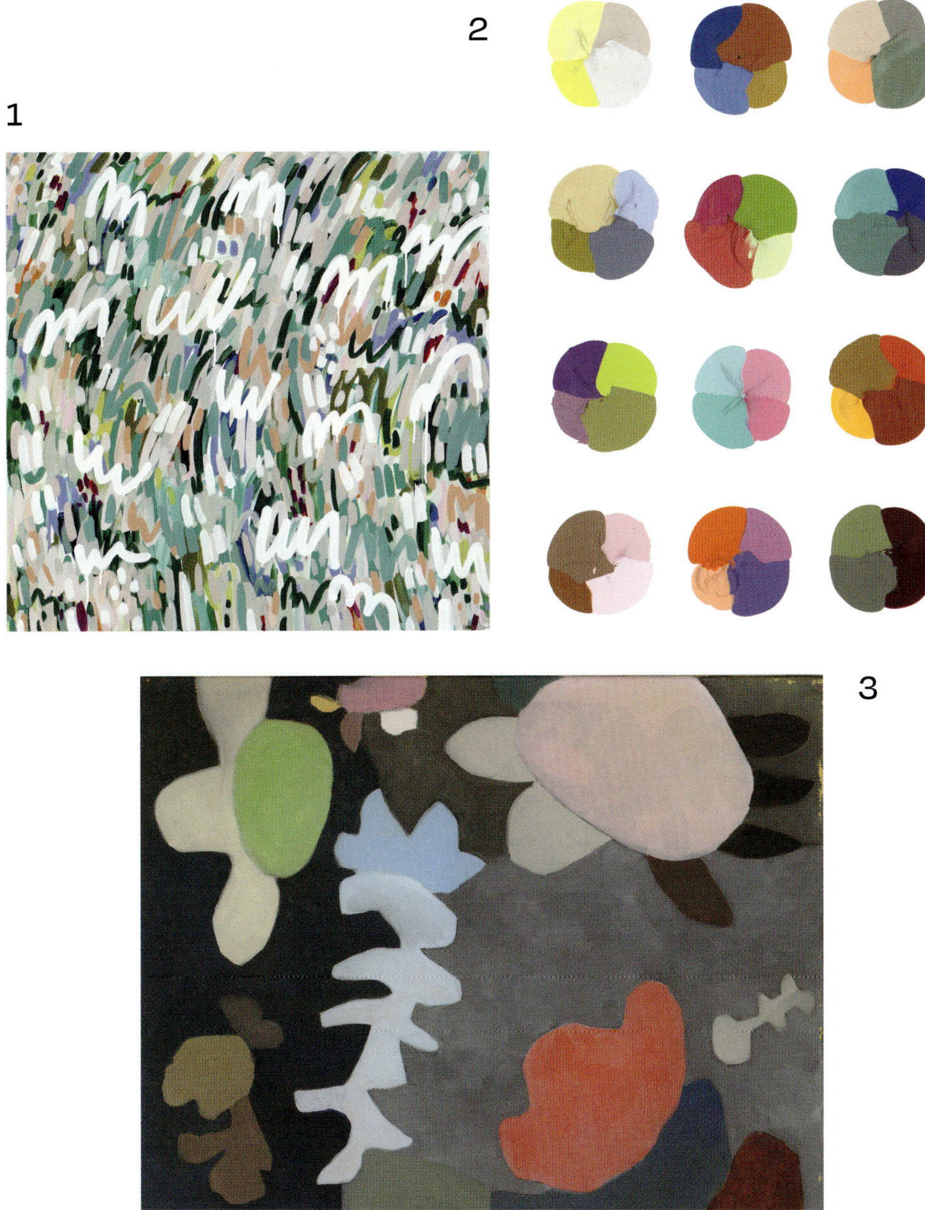
2
1
3

This page: Artwork, design, and photo by Racheal Jackson, Banyan Bridges. *Opposite:* Background artwork by Christina Flowers.

CHAPTER

BRING YOUR *Walls* TO LIFE

TWO

DOES ART HAVE TO HANG ON white walls?

Galleries traditionally have white walls and no furniture because they don't want anything to distract from the artwork. They create an environment that feels austere so that all attention goes to what is for sale. Your home, however, doesn't have to play by any rules. You can use color and pattern on the walls and showcase artwork by multiple artists. You're curating a life and a home, not an art show. I encourage you to play, and if your personal style veers more toward maximalist and color, I assure you it can all work together.

HOW CAN I add color TO MY WALLS?

When I am designing a room in my home, I look at it through the lens of art. I look for colors that can accentuate the artwork and pull out accent colors. I find it most interesting to play with secondary colors in a piece that will help me view the art in a new way. This, of course, means that you already own the artwork you are decorating with. There have been times I have repainted a room because of a new piece of artwork.

Opposite: Artwork by Angela Chrusciaki Blehm, Ashley Longshore, Cheryl Kellar, M. Negus, Mark Jackson, Jennifer Allevato, and vintage pieces. Design by Andrea Brooks Interiors. Photo by Mark Jackson / CHROMA. Background artwork by Theodora Miller.

Bottle Fed

BOLD COLOR

Color can change the mood and energy in a room. Oftentimes, people are afraid to use color because they believe it will feel overwhelming or that they will make the wrong choice. Paint color can make a room feel larger (or smaller), calmer (or more energetic), and inspiring (or bland). If you are color-curious, I have provided some of my favorite wall colors in the box to the right. These are colors we have used on accent walls in the gallery, and I have noticed these colors help so many pieces of art to stand out.

Using a color wheel is a helpful way to choose a color. If you have a prominent color in a work of art or piece of furniture, look at that color on a color wheel and then look to the opposite side of the wheel. If you have oranges in a work of art, look to blues for a wall color. Tone is also an important aspect of bringing multiple colors together. If you have a work of art with more muted colors, look for wall colors in that same scale of color to create a cohesive aesthetic throughout the room. Most important, though, you need to experiment. Take a work of art and a paint deck and play with the colors to see what feels best together. Paint is one of the easiest and fastest ways to make a room feel new. If you don't love the color, or you want a change, it's a simple fix. Remove the fear from design and move toward the joy.

LIZ'S FAVORITE PAINT COLORS TO DISPLAY ARTWORK

FARROW & BALL

NO. 234
Vert de Terre

NO. 9914
Sherbert Lemon

NO. 2004
Slipper Satin

SHERWIN WILLIAMS

7001
Pure White

6505
Atmospheric

6620
Rejuvenate

7048
Urbane Bronze

6187
Rosemary

BENJAMIN MOORE

1317
Yours Truly

HC-154
Hale Navy

This page: Artwork is vintage. Design by Elizabeth Rees. Photo by Anna Spaller. *Opposite:* Artwork by Rebecca Stern. Design by Molly Torres Portnof of DATE Interiors. Photo by Kirsten Francis.

Wallpaper

This is a personal favorite of mine because my style tends toward eclectic and layered. There are many, many options in the world of design, but here's my main rule of thumb: If your wallpaper features a bold color or pattern, go for artwork that is more minimal. If your wallpaper is more minimal, go with a bolder piece of art. Of course, rules are made to be broken, and I have seen bold wallpaper with bold artwork and it has worked. As style icon Iris Apfel always said, "More is more and less is a bore!"

AN ARTFUL CONVERSATION WITH

ELIZABETH REES

FROM CHASING PAPER

Elizabeth Rees is the co-founder of Chasing Paper, a premium wallcoverings brand based in Milwaukee, Wisconsin. Best known for innovating the removable wallpaper category with their fabric-based peel-and-stick wallpaper, Chasing Paper is a pioneer and leader in the home-décor industry, creating beautiful, clever solutions for the modern home.

Artwork is vintage. Design by Elizabeth Rees. Photo by Anna Spaller.

LIZ: Wallpaper has made a big comeback in recent years. Why do people use wallpaper to transform a room?

ELIZABETH: Wallpaper is such a powerful design tool because it instantly brings personality and warmth into a space. Whether it's a bold, statement-making print or a subtle texture, wallpaper allows you to create a mood and tell a story in a way that paint just can't. It's also a great way to define a space—especially in open-concept homes or smaller areas like entryways, bathrooms, or nooks where you want to make an impact. Plus, with peel-and-stick options, it's never been easier to experiment without a long-term commitment.

LIZ: Do you have any tips and tricks for people who want to pair artwork and wallpaper?

ELIZABETH: Absolutely! The key is balance. If you have a bold, patterned wallpaper, consider artwork with simpler lines or neutral tones so the two don't compete. On the flip side, if your wallpaper is more minimal, that's a great opportunity to layer in vibrant, textured, or oversize art to create a dynamic focal point. I also love playing with scale—mixing smaller, gallery-style frames with large-scale prints for a collected, intentional look. And don't forget about frames! Natural wood or metallic frames can add another layer of warmth and cohesion to the space.

LIZ: What do you consider when purchasing artwork for your own home?

ELIZABETH: I always look for pieces that feel personal—something that sparks joy, nostalgia, or inspiration. I love supporting independent artists, so I often browse local galleries or online shops for unique finds. A lot of the art in my home are also pieces I have found at vintage stores and flea markets: I love how something old has its own story and how it interacts with the rest of my home. Art is such a beautiful way to reflect your personality, and mixing styles, mediums, and even unexpected color combinations makes a space feel lived-in and layered. Most importantly, I believe you should always choose art you truly love rather than just following trends—it makes your home feel more like *you*.

Background artwork by Jennifer Allevato.

1 2

3 4

A STEP-BY-STEP GUIDE TO

hanging artwork on wallpaper

1.

Once you have determined where the artwork should be placed, mark an X in pencil on the wallpaper.

2.

Use a knife to create a small upside-down V cut around the X.

3.

Gently peel back so that the wallpaper is lifted from the wall.

4.

Place your nail directly into the wall.

OPTIONAL

If you ever move the artwork, you can use wallpaper paste (or even glue) to place the cut piece back into place.

Try it. I asked my framer to create a white mat for me for an artwork I was going to hang on wallpaper. I used spray glue on the mat and covered it with leftover wallpaper so that the piece would be framed in the wallpaper pattern. I then took the piece to the framer with the new mat and asked them to frame as usual. I love how the mat creates a conversation between the wallpaper and art and makes the pairing look even more intentional.

Opposite: Artwork by Megan Woodard Johnson.

Murals

A wall mural, meaning a painting that has been painted directly onto your wall, gives you the opportunity to play with scale and bring art into your home that goes beyond a simple frame or canvas. More and more artists are adding mural work to their services because it gives them the opportunity to go big and experiment in interesting ways. A mural also draws on the idea of an "accent wall" or focal point for a room, which is a fresh take on a traditional design element. As seen in the home of artist Racheal Jackson, her mural work layers perfectly with her work on canvas. Murals are customarily associated with the outdoors on the exterior of buildings, but bringing this large-scale art inside gives an opportunity to display really big style.

If you love the work of an artist but have a large or unusual space for artwork, a mural might be the right option. A mural could be one wall, all four walls, or even include the ceiling of a room. A mural artist uses your wall and space as their canvas. It's important to note, however, that not all artists will create a mural, and not all mural artists like to paint on smaller surfaces like canvas or paper. However, there is a Venn diagram of artists who like to create on canvas and also paint on walls.

While a piece of wall art is often priced by the square inch, with a mural we usually look at the price per square foot. Even if an artist whose work you love does not have wall murals in their current portfolio, I believe it's still worth asking politely. You can begin the conversation by asking their price per square foot and then apply that to your wall and budget accordingly. If you have a wall that is 8 feet tall and 10 feet wide, you have 80 square feet. Perhaps the artist's price per square foot is $30. So 80 sq. ft. x $30 is a wall mural price of $2,400. Murals can be a great "bang for your buck" due to their size and price while still creating a wonderful opportunity for an artist.

Murals and hand-painted décor elements can be used throughout your home—under door archways, around window molding, or as a substitute for traditional wallpaper borders. They also give you the opportunity to play with the "fifth wall" in a room: the ceiling!

Another option is to create a mural yourself. One of my main goals in life is to create more opportunities for artists, but I also believe that everyone (yes, *everyone*) has the ability to be artistic. I, personally, am happiest when I am working with my hands. You may feel that way too, and a mural wall may be a wonderful creative outlet for you.

Artwork and design by Angela Chrusciaki Blehm. Photo by Justin Salem Meyer.

AN ARTFUL CONVERSATION WITH

RACHEAL JACKSON

FROM BANYAN BRIDGES

Racheal Jackson is a muralist and designer who has made it her life's passion to recapture the freedom of color and creativity in people's homes. She paints murals in homes and businesses across the country under the name Banyan Bridges. Her work has been featured in Better Homes and Gardens, Flow *magazine,* Apartment Therapy, *and* Domino, *among other publications. Racheal is based in Vancouver, Washington.*

LIZ: You have built a career on incredible murals. What drew you to creating large-scale work in homes?

RACHEAL: I don't think there's an easier way to create drama than to use massive art. It instantly grounds a room by providing a focal point, creates a palette to play with the rest of the furnishings, and if done thoughtfully can also help balance any quirky or problematic architectural features.

LIZ: When deciding on a location for a mural, what do you consider?

RACHEAL: My first question is always "What problem are we solving?" Is it a long, narrow room that needs some width? Funky angles we don't know how to decorate? Maybe a vaulted stairwell that just stumps you. Murals are great tools for solving design problems.

LIZ: What are some key points you have learned when deciding whether a mural is right for a home?

RACHEAL: I'll always evaluate the space and try to use a mural to help with flow, focal point, and balance, but at the end of the day the deciding factor is really just "Do you want a mural?" If the answer is yes then we make it work!

Background artwork by Jennifer Allevato.

Artwork, design, and photo by Racheal Jackson.

Artwork by
Alex Ackerman.

HOW TO

create a mural

YOUR MAIN TOOLS WILL BE

- a computer
- design software like the Adobe Suite or Canva
- a projector
- a pencil
- a variety of sizes of paintbrushes
- paint

TIPS FOR CREATING A MURAL YOURSELF

1. ***If you are a novice designer/artist,*** I would recommend using a computer program to create a design or phrase that you would love to paint on your walls. Play with scale and fun fonts if you are using words in the design. Think of words or phrases that mean something special to your family or a song lyric you love. Don't be afraid to go big.

   - Once you have the design ready, turn off the lights and project onto the wall surface.
   - Lightly trace the design onto the wall. A light touch is important because you do not want the marks to be so thick the paint cannot cover them. Don't worry about the details so much yet while tracing.
   - Flip the switch back on and begin to paint within the lines. If there is detail work in the design you can repeat this process once the first layers of paint have dried.

2. ***If a pattern is more your speed,*** you can work with painter's tape or stencils to create the look. If you are using painter's tape in a mural, my number-one tip is to put the tape in place and then lightly paint over the edges with the background wall color. This helps seal the tape and create a crisp line. Then you can paint over with a contrasting color once the seal is dry. This was the technique I used in my entryway seen here.

HOW CAN I

pattern- and color-mix

LIKE A PRO?

Pattern- and color-mixing throughout your home and with art is not an exact science. Artwork can vary by style, artist, and medium, so whether you are bringing in multiple pieces of art or pairing one piece with a wallpaper or mural, the guidelines are the same.

The easiest way to mix prints is to play with patterns that are monochromatic. Using the same tone or patterns that have a similar color story throughout is a foolproof way to combine patterns. You do not need to stick to the exact same colors, but having even subtle colors carried throughout can help visually connect the artwork and patterns. Keeping artwork and colors in the same tone will make the design feel visually cohesive. Look for at least one unifying color, and the art and wallpaper will pair well together.

Vary the scale. Larger prints can handle busier or more detailed work. Smaller prints can handle bolder artwork. A variety of scales will prevent the design having too many elements competing for attention.

Play around with it! Do you like it? Does your gut tell you it works? Then it does! Trust it! Color and pattern bring joy into a home.

Opposite: Artwork by Shelby Monteverde.
Photo by Shelby Monteverde.

This page: Artwork by Donata Delano and other collected artists. Design by Orsi Panos. Photo by Patrick Biller Photography. *Opposite:* Background artwork by Christina Flowers.

CHAPTER

Art IS FOR EVERYONE

THREE

There's this myth that you have to be very wealthy to afford artwork, and I am on a mission to debunk it. When people picture an art-buying experience, too many of them think of wandering into a gallery and feeling unwelcome. The person behind the desk may be rude or not acknowledge you entirely. You may picture yourself looking at giant works of art (that quite frankly you do not "get") and there's not a price tag to be seen. There's a general feeling that if you have to ask how much artwork costs, then you can't afford it. What a terrible way to feel, and it's kept so many people away from the art world. Of course, that may be by design—fewer people in the art world could make it seem more elite—but I say, enough! The art world is vast and diverse and eclectic and no longer just for the chosen few. The art world is for everyone.

First and foremost, you are welcome in the art world. Allow me to be your welcome committee of one (although there are truly thousands of art world creatives who feel the same as I do). And second, there's such a wide range of artwork prices where, with planning, artwork can be within your reach. Everyone's budget is different, and in this chapter, I will be disclosing all the factors that go into the final price of a piece so that you can effectively budget and plan for your purchase. My hope is that by understanding the total price, you're able to determine what is affordable for you.

Background artwork by Kristen Abbott.

HOW DO ARTISTS

price their artwork?

First, you have the retail price of a piece. Artists price their work in a variety of ways, but often it is based on the price per square inch that they have established. Let's say an artwork is 10 × 20 inches. If an artist has an established price per square inch of $3, the formula would be this: 10 × 20 × 3= 600. So the price would be $600. This formula could be used to determine the price of any size of their work. Another way artists price their work is based on an hourly fee that they have determined is appropriate for their work, plus the price of any materials. This way is harder for a client to budget for future work because it is unknown how long a piece has taken an artist to create. I believe the cost-per-square-inch formula is the best, given the fact that artists will become faster as they perfect their technique.

Another thing to consider is commission if they are working with a gallery or retailer. A traditional commission for a piece from a gallery is 50 percent. That percentage can change based on the retailer or gallery due to a variety of factors. The gallery commission does not change the artwork's price. Pricing should stay consistent, whether you are purchasing from a gallery or directly from an artist. While the overall price is what matters most to the client, I find it helpful to "lift the curtain" so that you can understand how pieces are priced.

What other costs should you take into account?

SALES TAX: Be sure to factor in the sales tax for the gallery, which, of course, changes based on the location where the piece is being sold. It is appropriate to ask for an invoice that includes sales tax to understand the overall price.

SHIPPING: If the piece is being shipped to you, give the artist or gallery your zip code so that they can work with a shipping company or art handler to find the cost for you to receive the piece. An additional point to this price could also include needing a shipping crate to be built for any large pieces. You can typically plan for shipping to be about 10 percent of the artwork's price. Shipping insurance, which you can choose to include or not, is also a price consideration.

FRAMING: If the art being purchased is a work on paper, then you will also need to factor in the framing cost. You could ask the artist or gallery to handle this for you based on their recommendation, or you could work with a local framing company once the artwork has arrived. More on framing styles and the cost of framing in chapter eight.

INSURANCE: If the artwork is of a high value, you may want to reach out to your insurance provider to have the piece added to your home policy or have a specific rider created for it.

INSTALLATION: If you are not comfortable with installing an artwork—although I think you will be after chapter eight—you may hire an installer for your artwork. Many people who install artwork set their prices either by the artwork installed or on an hourly basis.

Not all of these hidden costs will apply to you each time you purchase an artwork. Let's take this hypothetical situation: You have a budget of $1,000 for artwork and you find a piece you love for $1,000. It's a painting on paper from a gallery across the country. The shipping is $100 if you have them send the artwork unframed. You receive the artwork and have it framed for $500. The true cost of the artwork, then, is $1,600, plus tax. Another scenario is that you purchase a work on canvas from a gallery in your city for $1,000. The artwork is ready to install, does not need framing, and the gallery has offered to deliver and install the artwork for you. The true cost of this artwork is $1,000 (plus tax). Hidden costs may take you outside of your budget quickly.

WHY IS ART SO expensive?

This is a question I receive a lot. The truth is most art is not so expensive. The artwork that makes the news headlines are the pieces that sell for millions of dollars at highly publicized international art auctions. When an artist you may have never heard of is selling work for more than $100 million, it makes many people feel like they can't even get close to purchasing an original artwork. But there's a whole other art world out there that consists of everyday people buying work at prices under $1,000, with the average price tag being $1,700. The Affordable Art Fairs that have annual events at locations around the world share the work of hundreds of artists and galleries for under $10,000. There are hundreds of art fairs around the world and specifically in the United States where artwork is priced around $100.

Now might be a good time to mention that what is affordable to one person is, of course, not affordable to another. When I talk about art and pricing, there is an inherent level of privilege involved. My point is to share that the art world includes many levels of pricing, not just what makes the headlines, and you can find artwork that fits your own personal level of investment if you do the research. My intent is to remain neutral about budget amounts, as I believe any support of an artist, regardless of the price, is a positive thing to encourage.

With all of that said, there are many factors that go into how an artwork is priced. I mentioned earlier the formulas involved for artists pricing a work, but here is more on how that price is determined.

SCARCITY AND DEMAND: If the artwork is an original work and there is no other work like it in the world, it creates a scarcity model. Additionally, if the artist is no longer creating new work (due to either retirement or being deceased), the scarcity increases because there are a finite number of works created by the artist. Supply and demand still exists while an artist is alive and currently working. Many artists only release a set number of works each year in order to not flood the market. Knowing that there are a limited number of opportunities, clients are willing to pay top dollar to acquire one of the pieces available.

ARTIST: The artist's career and place in the art-historical context can play a significant role in the pricing of an artwork. For example, Jackson Pollock plays a pivotal role in the abstract expressionist movement and therefore commands a significant sum of money for each of his paintings. On a smaller (but still important) scale, there are contemporary artists who are considered emerging artists or mid-career artists. Emerging artists are newer to the art world and have recently started selling their work, and their work often sees lower prices. A mid-career artist may have had their work in a museum or may have worked with significant galleries and so their work may see a higher price. An artist's reputation, as in many careers, helps them ask for higher prices.

PROVENANCE: This is a term that refers to a record of the ownership of an artwork and is used to prove authenticity. For example, if the provenance is not "tight" or clear on where an artwork resided for its entire history, it can call into question if that piece is legitimate. For many pieces, their provenance is quite simple. It might look something like this:

- Artist created the piece in their New York City studio.
- Artist shipped it to Liz Lidgett Gallery and it was received into inventory.
- Artwork was sold by the gallery to the client and it has resided in the client's home since.

Provenance is also important for the pricing of an artwork because it may show that a client loaned it to the Metropolitan Museum of Art for a show, showing historical significance, which would increase its value. Provenance can also help answer questions. About once a year, it seems that there is a news article where someone finds a significant piece of art by a famous artist at a garage sale. This is where provenance comes into play. What do we know about this piece? How would it have arrived where it is? From time to time, provenance proves the art is authentic. Perhaps a client dies and their family does not recognize the piece and so it's been sitting in an attic for thirty years before it shows up at a garage sale for $10. Provenance can be rediscovered by the right art appraisers if they are able to place it in an artist's studio or having been sold through a gallery. Then, all of a sudden, a $10 garage sale has significant value. Lack of provenance, meaning no information on the piece, can also harm an artwork's value because there will be no record to base the value of the work on or you may not be able to prove an artwork's authenticity.

QUALITY: Quality for an artwork can be tricky because beauty is in the eye of the beholder. What does not work for me may work well for you. I try to look at whether a piece is successful in its execution versus what is good or bad. This is where quality and craftsmanship can affect the price. If a work is meticulously created with specific materials, it will also increase the price. If the artist uses a technique that is very difficult to re-create or is time-intensive, this too can increase the price.

INVESTMENT: I believe you should buy artwork that you will love, and if, by chance, it happens to increase in value, then it is a lucky coincidence. However, if you would like to keep value and investment in mind, there are certainly artists who have shown a pattern of increasing value year over year. If you can get a sense of when an artist increases their prices, you could make a return on your investment in a matter of weeks. Research will be your friend here, whether by asking the artist directly or asking a gallery for a price pattern through the years.

Ultimately, though, art is not a good financial investment. I'd much rather you invest in your Roth IRA and just buy the pieces you love without thinking about making money down the line. The secondary market, meaning where a piece is being sold for the second (or third or fourth) time, is not stable. Many works of art do not hold their monetary value over time because it can be difficult to resell certain pieces. If you love the artwork, though, its value may be aesthetic or sentimental.

WHAT SHOULD I budget?

Clients often ask, "What should I budget for my first purchase?" This, of course, is a personal question. Ultimately only you can decide what feels comfortable for your wallet. If this is your first piece of artwork, making a budget of $1,000 to $2,500 can often help buyers feel at ease. Over time, as you continue to become more knowledgeable, you'll feel more confident in your purchases and you may want to invest more time and money in collecting. You will gain a better feel for what you like, your budget, and what goes into purchasing art. As with any new hobby, you won't know everything from the very beginning, and that's okay. Start small, lean on experts (and this book) at first, and you'll find your "sea legs" in the art world.

The secondary market

As discussed, the term "secondary market" refers to the situation where an artwork has already been sold once in the primary market and is now being sold again. While price can still run the gamut, if budget is of utmost concern, there are gems to be found on the secondary market. The secondary market can mean galleries that focus on reselling works, thrifting, auction houses, and even garage sales. The secondary market can also mean places like Christie's and Sotheby's that capture those headlines I spoke of. For our purposes in this book, I am focusing more on the regional auction houses and estate sales that can be found throughout the country. Take a look at the professional associations online that are affiliated with auction houses. These will be a great source for reputable, trusted sellers of artwork.

The opportunity to find a well-loved piece from another's collection can mean an opportunity to purchase the work well below the original owner's purchase price. It also means that you'll get to experience the thrill of the hunt, which is an added bit of fun.

The secondary market can also be filled with a range of challenges amidst all the opportunity. For sellers, determining the proper valuation and pricing of a work can be complex due to changing market trends, condition, and provenance. For example, if there is not a clear history of ownership and authenticity verification, an artwork may lose some of its value. Additionally, depending on the age of the piece, there can be certain kinds of deterioration that are acceptable but others that are not acceptable. Reselling art can also involve legal complexities, especially if there are resale rights/droit de suite. This can vary by country and even by state. I have seen it happen many times where a seller was the original buyer of the piece and remembers the sale price. They are then very surprised to see that the work, for any of the reasons above, is no longer valued at the original purchase price. Not all works hold or appreciate in value, so the demand for an artist's work can certainly shift based on the current market and trends. In fact, some pieces may be worth almost nothing in terms of money, but I'd argue that the artwork still has value—*aesthetic* value.

For buyers, the secondary market also brings some risks to think through. Forgeries or misattributions can make working with an expert essential. All of the same concerns listed for sellers apply with regard to provenance and condition, of course, just on the receiving end. Budget-wise, the secondary market also can come with high transaction costs for the buyer, depending on how you are purchasing the work.

Although there are these pitfalls to consider before purchasing, there are also many pros. Artwork that you buy and sell on the secondary market has established a purchase history, so you are able to see if a piece has increased in value compared to when it was a primary sale. This can help you estimate whether the artwork could potentially continue to increase in value in the future. There are no guarantees in the art world, but an established history can help predict future trends.

If you are hoping to sell a piece of art in the secondary market, your best bet is to call multiple established sources, such as secondary market galleries and auction houses. Depending on the piece and any value information you have (like from an appraisal), you may need to look at either regional or international institutions. If the aesthetic value is high but you do not have information about the artist or provenance, it can be difficult to get a financial value on a piece. That's when antique and vintage stores focusing more on design than art may be a good bet for your sale.

AN ARTFUL CONVERSATION WITH

GILLIAN BRYCE

OWNER OF GILLIAN BRYCE GALLERY

Gillian says of herself, "I don't remember a time when art—either the creation of or the enjoyment of—didn't take me to a place where all was right with the world. A deep and private place I could call my own, where my thoughts and intentions were focused solely on the aesthetic."

LIZ: Please tell us about your role in the secondary market as a dealer.

GILLIAN: I've always been fascinated with the past and the art movements of the twentieth century. I became passionate about collecting works by artists who had passed as a way of preserving their legacy. As my career progressed, I discovered and acquired lifetime portfolios of artists whose works were exceptional and yet they had somehow escaped the recognition of the art market during their time.

I'm determined to ensure that the artists who have gone before us have their stake in the art world.

I'm lucky to have the client base that I have. I work closely with not only incredible interior designers, from celebrity designers to start-up firms, but with collectors at all levels. I love nothing more than helping new collectors starting out in their journey to be excited about art.

My gallery model is much different than the typical contemporary market in that I purchase outright and own all of my inventory. All of the artists whose life's work that I own actually become a part of my family in a sense. I display their pictures and have to think that they would be happy to see the incredible responses that their art evokes.

LIZ: How do you find the work that you sell?

GILLIAN: When I started out and was just building inventory, I would go just about anywhere. Thrift stores, estate sales, antique stores and shows, social media sites. As my client base and demand has grown exponentially, I rely on a trusted group of dealers who source art for me coast to coast, both by the piece and by the portfolio. I'm very particular and largely only acquire works that I would want to hang in my own collection.

LIZ: What are a few important tips for those interested in purchasing from a secondary market dealer?

GILLIAN: Find dealers whose aesthetics you are drawn to and who have a solid reputation. Be sure to buy art that you love and don't be persuaded to purchase art simply for financial gain. Trust your gut, both in what you want to live with and who you feel good about doing business with. It's a much simpler and more enjoyable process when you work with a dealer you trust and respect.

Hot Tip: While I am shopping for art, I have a note on my phone that includes a photo of the room I want to buy a piece for, size measurements of both the wall and any furniture near the proposed space, and a list of any wishes or wants. This list helps me stay focused on what would work well for the space, and not just on the fact that the piece may be a bargain.

If I find an artwork that works well, I look all around the piece to make sure that it is in good condition. Is the frame intact? If it is a work on paper, is there any discoloration to the artwork? Damage to an artwork can happen through too much light exposure, moisture, and age. "Foxing" is a term that refers to the small red-and-brown splotches that can appear on a piece of paper over time if the paper is not of high quality. However, if there are works that have damage, you can determine if it is something that still works well with the overall style and look. For example, I purchased a small piece in France at an outdoor thrift market. The piece has some browning and even a rip on the canvas. Nevertheless, it hangs above our bed and it makes me think of that wonderful trip. When you're thrifting, I believe you can focus more on the gut reaction of loving a piece rather than the value of a piece.

Background artwork by Jennifer Allevato.

IS EVERYONE getting a discount BUT ME?

The answer is no and yes and maybe. Discounts are one of those highly controversial yet common things that help to make the art world feel very cloak-and-dagger. The truth is that the majority of artwork that we sell personally at my gallery is without discount. We do work with interior designers who often receive something called a "trade discount," which is a small percentage off the price that designers also receive at furniture retailers, for example, to encourage their business. Occasionally, a small number of our loyal and repeat customers will receive a small discount (around 10 percent) to help offset shipping and so on. The truth is also that discounts do happen often throughout the art world and are often based on relationships. Some galleries may offer a discount to a museum, for example, or to another collection where they would like an artist's work to have a place. Artists and galleries both occasionally offer discounts based on an existing relationship with a supportive client. If you are a first-time buyer, it's appropriate to enter into the conversation with respect and understand that your purchase most likely will not receive a discount. Some clients feel like a discount should be a "given," like a retail price is a suggestion, and that's truly a myth. Discounts do happen, but not always.

Opposite: Artwork by Fares Micue. Design by Toledo Geller Interiors. Photo by Jacob Snavely Photography.

This page: Artwork by Kristen Abbott. Design and photo by Annabode Interior Design.
Opposite: Background artwork by Christina Flowers.

CHAPTER

LET'S Buy SOME ART!

FOUR

I have had many clients through the years with large walls. A really common issue is that the client's budget doesn't match the size of the wall. This is an excellent example of being creative with your purchases and installations while you are working your way toward what you want. Your collection will grow over time as you fall in love with art. It all starts with your first purchase.

You know your style, your space, and your budget. You feel ready to have the conversation and you know what questions you want to ask. It's time to buy some art!

This page: Art and design by Kristie McGowan. Photo by Cat Wilborne Photography. *Opposite:* Background artwork by Kristen Abbott.

WHERE CAN YOU

Buy Art?

There are many places to buy art around the world. The list below includes the most common places.

Buy from an Art Gallery

As an art gallery owner, I'll be the first person to tell you that not all art galleries operate the same way. When you're looking for an art gallery, doing your research is an important part of the process. Make sure to take the time to look them up online and peruse their website beforehand. Having a list of the artists you like that the gallery works with can be very helpful in your conversations with them.

There are many stereotypes about what it is like to walk into an art gallery. Do you picture walking into a cold, quiet, white space? Do you picture a gallerista in all black clothing not-so-silently judging you with her eyes? Do you feel nervous because there are no prices on any of the artwork so you're not sure if you can afford it? I'm here to tell you that while those places do exist, the majority of galleries are welcoming, artful, creative places. Your research beforehand will be key, because you'll have an idea of the gallery's aesthetic and overall vibe. Look for a gallery where you will feel comfortable and that carries the work of artists you like. You can get a feel for this by looking through the websites and social media of multiple galleries. Pay attention to their tone and voice. For example, do they feel approachable? Are you seeing multiple artists whose work speaks to you? It's important to note here that if you begin to collect art without favorite artists in mind, that's OK! You can find the styles and artists that speak to you over time as you peruse galleries.

Many galleries work differently but most should have pricing readily available for you. If the prices and information are not directly shown on the wall, ask for a "price list," which will share the title and price of each piece printed on a piece of paper for you to walk around with.

The next step will be to have a conversation with someone who works in the gallery. This would be the time to share photos and dimensions of your space and ask any questions about the artist. If you feel comfortable with the purchase, now would be the time to buy your work of art. If you still have questions, ask for the gallery's contact information. It's more than OK to walk away at this time, but understand that the work may be sold if you change your mind later. If you're local, many galleries allow you to bring the artwork to your home to test the placement of the art. If you're not local, you may ask if the gallery offers digital placement services, meaning they may be able to mock up the artwork into a photo of your space.

While you are perusing a gallery, notice that if there is a red dot on a label next to a piece, that piece is sold. This is a common way for galleries to notify clients that the piece is no longer available.

If you're not able to physically go to the gallery space, many people buy artwork online without ever seeing the piece in person. If you feel uncomfortable with this, I'd recommend calling and speaking to someone over the phone about the piece. The art world has changed in the past few years to the point where you are able to purchase online through the art gallery's website. My clients often ask for a short video to be sent to them as well. Videos are a great tool that can show how an artwork lives in a physical space. A photo doesn't always show the scale or texture of an artwork as well as a video can.

Opposite: Artwork by Katie Craig.

WERNER

Buy Directly from an Artist

Another more recent development in the art world includes artists selling directly to clients and sidestepping the traditional gallery model. Of course, there have always been artists who have sold on their own, but for decades the tradition has been for an artist to graduate with a Master of Fine Arts (an MFA) and then sign a contract with a gallery. This is what artists have been told makes them a "legitimate artist" for a very long time. Now, though, the internet and social media have democratized the art world in new ways and artists are able to reach a much wider audience directly. Many successful artists no longer go to MFA programs and some are self-taught. Instagram has been a leading way for artists to find their audiences and a great tool for selling artwork. Getting to know an artist and their work through social media also helps you understand more about their technique and aesthetic.

Many artists now sell their artwork directly through their websites or Instagram. If an artwork is not available, it is appropriate to reach out to the artist to ask when their next collection of work will be created and shared. Additionally, they may be open to creating commissions if they do not currently have the piece you are looking for or the size you would like.

Bidding at Auction

Artwork can also be purchased at auction. Most of the time, the artwork at auction is being sold on the secondary market, meaning not directly from an artist or gallery. This also means that the artwork sale proceeds will be split between the owner of the artwork and the auction house. Auction sale prices are often the sale prices that make the news for the multi-million-dollar price tags. However, there are thousands more regional and local auction houses that can be excellent sources of artwork found at a great price. If you have a specific artist in mind who is no longer creating artwork (because they have passed or retired), an auction house is a great place to check because a previous owner may be downsizing their own collection.

Opposite: Artwork and design by Angela Chrusciaki Blehm and vintage.
Photo by Justin Salem Meyer. Background artwork by Theodora Miller.

When purchasing at auction, it's important to know what the final price will be. The "hammer price" includes what you bid to purchase the artwork and then in most cases a "buyer's premium" will be added to the hammer price. The buyer's premium is what the auction house charges in addition to the hammer price, and it can be somewhere between 10 percent and 30 percent. On top of this, there may be a shipping fee as well if the auction house is not local to you.

There are two main ways to purchase from an auction house: in person and online.

In-person auctions can be for either a smaller, regional company or a larger, international company. Before the auction, the houses will publish a catalog listing the artworks, descriptions, and estimated price ranges. You will want to review the catalog beforehand for any research needed and to set your game plan. If there are works you want to bid on, you can request a preview and/or a condition report. This report gives a more detailed description of the piece and assesses its authenticity and quality. You will also want to preregister with the auction house and receive your bidding number. During the auction, the auctioneer will begin with an opening bid—often this bid will be lower than the estimated price. Bidders will raise their paddles to signal a bid, but some houses will also accept absentee bids with preset maximum bids. Picture any auction scene in a movie and it will probably be similar to that. Bidding at an in-person auction is a rush, and my advice is to go into the experience with a set and firm budget number. If you get a steal that's wonderful, but it's also easy to be swept up in the excitement and adrenaline of outbidding someone else.

For an online art auction, there are a few different scenarios that may take place. Some auction houses offer online bidding that goes in tandem with the in-person auction. If you're not able to attend the auction in New York or Tokyo, you can watch from the comfort of your own home and bid electronically. Additionally, many auction houses also have the capability to set up an online auction through a website that ends at a predetermined time (similar to eBay).

If you win a piece at an auction (online or in-person), there will be a payment request issued with the final price of the piece, which includes the hammer price and any additional fees. Most likely this will be automatic because many auctions require your payment information before you are able to bid. Finally, they will arrange for shipping or pickup when appropriate.

Buy from an Antique Store or Thrifting

Buying from an antique dealer or thrifting can be a perfect way to pick up something fun and unexpected for a lower cost. I like to set a limit like $50 or $100 for artwork I find while thrifting. Of course, there are rare moments where you may find an artwork that will end up on *Antiques Roadshow* for $100,000, but as we discussed, when thrifting you will mostly find works that have aesthetic value, not monetary. Only you can determine what is right for your space and your wallet. My rule of thumb is to set a hard price limit unless you find a unicorn of a piece. This way, if I am spending larger amounts of money I know that my dollars are going to directly support an artist and a small business.

While thrifting (and this goes for art, objects, and furniture) I love to use Google Lens in the Google app on my phone. The lens will quickly bring up other art or items like the piece I have found and can potentially give me more information if there isn't any context.

Artwork and photo by Susannah Carson.

IMPORTANT THINGS TO NOTICE WHEN YOU ARE

THRIFTING OR ANTIQUING FOR ARTWORK

1 Check to see if you can see the artist's signature, or if there is any information about the artist or gallery on the back of the piece.

2 Look at how the piece is hung and the stability of the frame, if there is one. Is this a piece that is ready to hang, or will it require work?

3 Take a close look at the aging of the piece, and if there is any damage or discoloration. Has there been fading due to light or any moisture if the piece is on canvas or paper?

4 If you are unsure of the material, look at the texture of the piece. A common technique for lower-cost, mass-produced works is to have a print on canvas with an overlay of gesso or coating to re-create the look of brushstrokes. Oil paint will have more texture, for example, so get up close to the piece. It's also very fair to ask someone at the store about the piece and if they know anything about it.

5 If the piece is a print, look to see if there is a signature, an edition number, or the letters AP for artist's proof. A watermark or an embossment can give you information about the printer or publisher who distributed the print. A COA may also be present and attached to the piece with more information.

6 Personal connection is the most important part of shopping for art while thrifting. If the piece ends up being a hidden, underpriced gem, that just happens to be an added benefit. Buy what you love and you will not be disappointed.

AN ARTFUL CONVERSATION WITH

VIRGINIA CHAMLEE

AUTHOR OF *BIG THRIFT ENERGY*

Virginia Chamlee is a writer, artist, antiques dealer, and author of the bestselling book Big Thrift Energy. *She also authors a Substack newsletter about shopping for vintage art and interiors, called What's Left.*

LIZ: What do you look for when thrifting for artwork?

VIRGINIA: I am always on the hunt for original artwork and specifically abstract and contemporary works. I love anything large-scale that makes a big impact. I am drawn to anything with a bit of whimsy. And I particularly love thrifting in cities that are home to art colleges (think Savannah, Georgia, or Providence, Rhode Island). Art students will often donate huge chunks of their portfolios to thrift stores.

LIZ: Is there anything you would stay away from when thrifting?

VIRGINIA: I stay away from anything there's too much of. People often mistake artwork that is mass produced and printed on canvas as original art. A simple reverse Google image search can go a long way and ensure that what you're buying is actually original and not a factory-made piece.

LIZ: What are your tips for negotiating the price of thrifted objects and artwork?

VIRGINIA: Most thrift stores (particularly nonprofit stores) are charitable endeavors so negotiating artwork at those shops isn't always feasible. But certainly at an antique gallery or flea market, you should make an offer. It's important to be respectful to the dealer (I wouldn't offer more than 20 percent off the listed price), but also keep in mind that if it's been on the floor long, or if it's the final day of a yard sale or flea market, they are likely to be more eager to part with it.

LIZ: What's your favorite piece of artwork that you have thrifted?

VIRGINIA: I found an incredible Warrington Colescott artist's proof at a Habitat Re:Store in Jacksonville, Florida. It was produced in 1966 and is titled *Wall Street* and depicts stock traders in New York. The subject matter is subversive and only fifty were made (one of which is in the Museum of Modern Art's permanent collection).

LIZ: Anything else you want to talk about when thrifting art?

VIRGINIA: Anything that I maybe missed? Thrifting is a great opportunity to expand or begin an art collection because the work is very affordable and there's something for everyone, from sculpture to photography. Keep an eye out for the "weird" stuff, which many people pass by but is often the most unique and valuable.

Background artwork by Jennifer Allevato.

Buy at an Arts Festival or Art Fair

An arts festival or market and an art fair have major similarities and differences, so let's review! An arts festival is often produced by a nonprofit organization. There is often a jury of curators that review each application submitted by an artist and specific artists are invited to sell their work. When you attend a festival, they're often set up so that there are long rows of tents (often outside) and the artist is there selling their work. This is a great time to see a lot of art quickly and get to connect with artists.

An art fair is often put together by a for-profit entity and galleries or artists purchase a booth (often indoors) and they can bring the work by multiple artists that they represent. Art fairs are often in large warehouses or convention centers, where the galleries are able to create cube-like structures that try to mimic their actual galleries in a smaller setting. Clients/fair-goers usually interact with gallery employees and not the artists themselves in these instances.

Both festivals and fairs are great locations to see what artists are working on, spot major trends, and absorb a lot of artwork at once. I prefer to do a lap first, quickly reviewing the work of each tent or booth with the map in hand. I star any artist or gallery that piques my interest and this gives me a route to review in my second lap.

Both are also great opportunities to research artists or galleries that you like, even if you are not going to purchase on that specific day. I always leave a fair with a notebook full of business cards and contact information. Additionally, most galleries and artists release new work through newsletters, and I usually sign up for them in person in their booth.

Art markets are smaller, less formal ways to see many local artists. I love to look on community calendars for art markets that are sometimes held at makers' studios or even breweries. Even when I am traveling, I do a quick Google search for a city's community calendar to see what I can find when I am visiting.

Opposite: Artwork and design by Angela Chrusciaki Blehm and vintage. Photo by Justin Salem Meyer.

This page: Artwork by Hunt Slonem, Paige Barnes Dorsey, Betsy Enzensberger, Elsie Larson, Bethany Mabee, Hillary Howorth, and Emily Keating Snyder. *Opposite:* Background artwork by Katie Craig.

HOT TIP

It's appropriate to look for signage about taking photos of artwork at any festival or fair. Some artists and galleries welcome photography, others do not. If you do not see any signage, it's okay to ask! "Is it okay to take photos in your booth so I can review the pieces with my spouse?" "Is it okay to take photos in your booth? I am sharing artists I like on my Instagram!" Artists appreciate the conversation and your courtesy of asking, so I always default to "just ask!"

AN ARTFUL CONVERSATION WITH

AMELIA MANDERSCHEID

FOUNDER OF LEGACY ART PARTNERS

Amelia Manderscheid is the founder of Legacy Art Partners, a full-service boutique art advisory firm. She has more than fifteen years' experience in the art world, previously at Christie's in New York and Bonhams in San Francisco. She has an MBA from Columbia Business School and a BA in economics and art history from Wellesley College.

LIZ: What are some benefits to working with an art adviser?

AMELIA: An art adviser's job is to help steer the ship of the art-collecting journey. They can help expose collectors to new artists, negotiate better terms for sales or purchases, and ensure that, in our busy world, the collector's vision is carried out and that they are able to live with and enjoy their art collection.

LIZ: Who should work with an art adviser? Are there any ideal or preferred characteristics for a client?

AMELIA: Anyone who is seriously considering starting an art collection and is not sure where to begin, anyone who has built a substantial collection and needs help managing it, and anyone who is considering selling a large number of works is someone who should work with an art adviser. An art adviser can be like a real estate agent; they help to locate and secure works, negotiate contracts, and act as an advocate, but ultimately it is the individual who is collecting whose taste the collection should reflect.

LIZ: **Can you tell us about a success story?**

AMELIA: One success story I would love to share was about someone who was new to collecting art, had just had their home remodeled, and had saved a few ideas for their collection but did not know how to acquire works or what they cost. I was able to connect them with the galleries that featured the works they were interested in, monitor the upcoming auction sales, and introduce them to new artists they didn't know. Now ten years later, they are the ones introducing me to new artists! I also wanted to note that there are many great original artworks out there priced between $2,000 and $50,000. The media only publishes the biggest prices but the vast majority of sales happen in this price range.

LIZ: **Anything else you want to add about working with an art adviser?**

AMELIA: Basically if you feel intimidated or overwhelmed by a facet of collecting art, an adviser is there to act as the gateway to art collecting. Also everyone charges fees differently. There really is no industry standard, so feel free to work with people on a one-time, case-by-case, or long-term basis. Collecting art is about relationships–and the art itself!–so an adviser is just another relationship to add into the mix.

Background artwork by Jennifer Allevato.

SHOULD YOU WORK WITH AN

art adviser?

There are benefits to working with an art adviser as you continue to collect. Art advisers help collectors select art to purchase through researching and analyzing options from a large variety of sources. Advisers are able to work with any artist or gallery and are not limited because they do not represent artists. As an independent entity, they can be flexible with their suggestions. Drawbacks can be that art advisers make a percentage of any purchase that the client makes. This percentage is agreed upon between client and adviser at the beginning of the relationship, and it is sometimes paid from the gallery or can be added to the price of purchase. Additionally, there may be retainer fees before purchasing work. There are many art advisers out there because there is no official credential needed.

The reasons to work with an adviser center around efficiency and access. Advisers can be quite knowledgeable about available artwork and clients often see this as a major benefit because it speeds up the art buying process. Additionally, there are certain galleries that prefer to work with an adviser and, based on their reputation, may offer artwork to an adviser that they would not normally make available.

Working with an adviser is not necessary to begin collecting. While there are many terrific art advisers at each budget level, I believe that working with a trusted gallery or designer to begin is the right option. If you decide over time that you want to invest heavily in artwork, passing the six-figure mark regularly, then working with an adviser should be considered.

Opposite: Artwork by Elisa Sheehan.
Interior design by Top Rail Interiors, LLC.
Photo by Elizabeth Haynes Photography.

WHAT DO YOU DO ONCE YOU HAVE purchased A WORK OF ART?

Once you have purchased a work of art, request an invoice that can be saved physically or digitally for your records. Some artists and galleries like to provide a certificate of authenticity along with a work of art as well, but it is not always used. A gallery can generate a CoA that also works alongside the invoice they give you.

Also request any information about the artist, the gallery, or the show that the piece was included in. Many galleries will create an artist bio sheet for each artist or a pamphlet or book for a gallery show. Remember to take a business card from the gallery or sales associate you worked with. You may have questions down the line and this way you won't have to rely on just your memory of that one side street in Rome you walked down and found your favorite painting. All of this information helps to build the provenance of the work and will make future appraisals much easier. If you do the upfront work, your future self will thank you. Documentation of a purchase is something most people do not think about until it's too late. All it takes is a simple file folder or two to hold this information.

If you keep your documentation, you will be ready for future appraisals, sales, and those moments you can't remember the artist's name.

Additionally, within one calendar year, you can send the artwork invoice to your insurance so they can properly document the purchase. Past a calendar year, in most cases, you will need to work with a fine art appraiser on an appraisal of the artwork or collection. A Certificate of Authenticity will also work if it shows the purchase price and date.

Opposite: Background artwork by Kevin Brent Morris.

HOT TIP

If you need to have the artwork framed, you can ask your framer to create a pocket on the back of the frame to keep any documentation. This is where I keep CoAs, invoices, business cards from the gallery or artist, and any personal notes from the artist.

ART ETIQUETTE!

If you have been working with a gallery and they introduce you to an artist, the best business practice is to go through that gallery for a commission. Galleries are small businesses that work hard to market their artists. If they have been great to work with, reward them by continuing your business with them. Many artists have a clause in their contract that requires them to bring previous gallery client commissions through the gallery. Sometimes the artist does not know, though! Help the artist and the gallery by continuing to work with them.

WHEN DO YOU NEED AN

appraisal?

There are several reasons why a client may want to request an appraisal. Look online for a listing of reputable art appraisers in your area through organizations like the International Society of Appraisers (ISA) and the Appraisers Association of America (AAA). Most appraisers will charge a flat fee per artwork that needs to be appraised. Do not work with an appraiser who charges a percentage of the artwork's worth. In no way should an appraiser be invested in how much the work is valued.

In order for an appraiser to begin finding the value of an artwork, they must know the reason for the appraisal. These are some of the reasons why a client may need an appraisal:

INSURANCE COVERAGE: To properly cover an artwork, many insurance companies will require a recent appraisal. Work with your agent to figure out the best way to insure your artwork. You may want to add the artwork to your homeowner's or renter's policies. Depending on the value of the work, you may want to work with a specialized fine art insurance.

DONATIONS FOR TAX DEDUCTIONS: This type of appraisal is needed if you will be gifting an artwork to a 501(c)(3) nonprofit organization. In addition to creating an appraisal for your donation, the appraiser will most likely also need to sign form 8283 if you are working with an accountant. That form covers non-cash charitable contributions.

ESTATE PLANNING OR INHERITANCE: An appraisal for inheritance or estate planning is helpful for tax valuation or for a fair division of assets once a loved one has passed.

BUYING OR SELLING ART: This type of appraisal is where the appraiser will look for the fair market value (FMV). FMV is the amount of money an artwork would yield if the artwork was sold in an open, competitive market, without duress (such as a need for a quick sale). Many times, clients will request an appraisal for FMV out of curiosity. They may not have decided they are ready to sell an artwork, but they are interested in knowing if their investment has grown in value. It's also helpful to get an appraisal if you are thinking about purchasing an artwork from a source outside of a gallery you trust or an auction house. An example could be purchasing an artwork from a friend or family member. An appraisal takes the emotion out of the purchase and creates facts using prior sales of other similar works.

It is important for the appraiser to understand the need for the appraisal because the values may differ depending on the purpose. The FMV finds what an artwork would sell for on the current market. An insurance appraisal looks for the replacement value, which can be higher than FMV because it reflects the retail price at a gallery or dealer. The secondary market (or FMV) can be lower than the original sale price at which an artwork was previously sold. The paperwork and documentation that you secure from the original purchase will help the appraiser create a better and more accurate picture of current value.

Artwork by Hunt Slonem and Paige Barnes Dorsey.

This page: Artwork by Etta Ehrlich. *Opposite:* Background artwork by Christina Flowers.

CHAPTER

NO MORE Blank WALLS

FIVE

Can any piece of art go anywhere? One of my favorite stories from my days studying art history is all the locations the *Mona Lisa* had lived before it ended up in the Louvre. Famously, Leonardo da Vinci traveled with the painting toward the end of his life. Once he died, Leonardo's apprentice and lover, a man named Salai, inherited the *Mona Lisa*. Salai then sold it to the French king. The king then hung the painting . . . in his bathroom. The *Mona Lisa* was a piece of bathroom art for almost a century until Louis XIV took the painting to the Palace of Versailles. It then hung in Napoleon's bedroom (such a versatile piece) for a short stint before it made its way to its permanent home—the Louvre Museum in Paris.

Is every piece the *Mona Lisa*? Obviously not, but I think the lesson of the provenance of Leonardo's most famous piece is that art can go anywhere, from a king's throne room (both kinds of thrones) to the most humble of locations. As long as it's placed with care and serves a purpose, even if that's the owner's happiness, art belongs.

This page: Background artwork by Kristen Abbott. *Opposite:* Artwork by Katie Craig and Jose Romussi.

LET THERE

be light

(BUT NOT TOO MUCH)

In the next section we will break all rules down by specific room, but light exposure is something to think about for any room in your home. Exposure to too much light while an artwork is on display will damage the piece. The material of an artwork and how the piece is framed matter when it comes to light. A work on paper can be easily damaged while a piece on metal is harder to damage. To determine if an artwork is light sensitive, it is worth having a conversation with the artist or gallery. If that is not possible, it is best to assume that the piece should not be exposed to direct sunlight. UV glazing will help protect from some light exposure compared to an unprotected piece. Light damage is cumulative, meaning each time the artwork is exposed to harsh lighting, further discoloration or fading will occur, and over time this will create major changes. To help prevent this, make sure that your art is never in direct sun exposure. Take a look at how your room changes throughout the day and how the sun comes in through the windows. Even direct sun exposure for a few minutes each day will take its toll.

Curators and conservationists have found that specific colors (like blue) and mediums (works on paper) are more susceptible to light damage. On page 210 I talk about how to light a piece of artwork inside a room. If you do have a large wall in need of artwork that does get sun exposure, I'd suggest looking for a work on wood or metal. Finding a piece with a more durable material will help prevent damage.

Opposite: Background artwork by Daisy Faith.

HOT TIP

There is a specific glazing (the piece of acrylic used in framing an artwork) that blocks ultraviolet light radiation. This helps protect a work on paper tremendously. Usually, works on paper, such as a watercolor painting or a photograph, are pieces that are framed with glazing. Canvases, when framed, are often framed using a float frame without glazing so texture can be seen.

Kitchen

What to consider

Let's first consider the function of your kitchen. If you are a gourmet cook who is a workhorse in the kitchen, you will have different considerations than, say, Carrie Bradshaw, who stored her sweaters in her oven. If you are the type of cook where flour is thrown around the room and oil splatters do happen, then there are some additional artwork considerations. Material and durability are two important factors when it comes to choosing your piece. Many types of artwork, such as works on paper and works on canvas, can absorb smoke, smells, and other debris that are common by-products in kitchens. If your artwork could at any point be splashed, you'll want to look for works of art that are protected through glass or acrylic or are made from a material such as tile or metal that is easily wipe-able. If you have a valuable piece of artwork, you may want to look at another room for the display or, at the very least, keep it away from the work area.

Here, interior designer Andrea Brooks placed an artwork by Gina Julian on her stove hood to add a pop of color to her gorgeous, neutral kitchen. The piece is high enough from the working surfaces that it is out of harm's way while offering the perfect amount of surprise to a more traditional space.

Opposite: Artwork by Gina Julian.
Design by Andrea Brooks Interiors.
Photo by Mark Jackson / CHROMA.

WHAT WORKS WELL

- Framed artwork that can be easily wiped
- Metal artwork, such as photography printed on aluminum
- Smaller artworks that can hang in nooks and crannies around the room. They also can look wonderful leaning or sitting on shelves alongside your bowls and plates.
- Using secure hanging methods as artwork is susceptible to vibrations, such as closing cabinets. I like to use a small amount of museum putty in the lower corners to secure the frames to prevent them going askew.

SUBJECT MATTER

- Anything goes but think about what you do in a kitchen: eat and drink! Fun ways to play on this theme would be artwork such as Elisa Sheehan's pieces made of eggshells or table scenes showing a beautiful meal or fruit.

INSPIRATION FOR KITCHEN

- On your oven vent (if it has a wood surround)
- Above windows, higher near the ceiling
- Lower on a wall near a pet's eating area. A cheeky way to create some design for pets too!
- Along your backsplash. Depending on the weight of the piece, an adhesive hook works well on tile!

Artwork by Brian Burt. Design by Gina Julian. Photos by Shannon Fontaine.

ABOVE: This small collection in a kitchen that peeks into a dining room goes on theme with delicious treats ready to be devoured. BELOW: A collection of vintage and collected plates.

Bathroom

What to consider

Not all bathrooms are built the same, of course. A powder room, for example, is not exposed to the same amount of steam and moisture as a full bathroom. If your bathroom does not have a bath or shower, anything goes! For our purposes, the notes below are under the assumption that you'll be taking lovely steamy baths next to the artwork. Ventilation and an exhaust fan are your artwork's friends here to help reduce the moisture in the air.

Here we worked with artist Paige Barnes Dorsey on a commission for a client to play off her lovely floral wallpaper. Smaller water closets can have big style, such as this busy wallpaper pattern and the hand-painted sink. Paige's snake looks right at home crawling on the garden-like wall but also happens to be a great material for the room, with glazed clay that can be cleaned when necessary.

Opposite: Artwork by Paige Barnes Dorsey.

Artwork by Anne Darby Parker, Stacey Spangler, and Alex Bodishbaugh King. Design by Andrea Brooks Interiors. Photo by Mark Jackson / CHROMA.

WHAT WORKS WELL

- Artwork on tile
- Artwork on metal, such as aluminum or mid-century modern brass pieces
- A gallery wall of beautiful baskets or other textile work

WHAT DOESN'T WORK AS WELL

- Artwork on paper or canvas. These are all materials that absorb moisture and can become warped over time.

SUBJECT MATTER

- Bathrooms are a great place to play with subject matter, such as figurative or nudes. One large piece or a collection of smaller nudes can be a celebration of the human body while being very sophisticated. Soothing abstracts can also give the illusion that you have a spa in your very own home. Think calming blues, greens, and neutrals in your abstracts.

INSPIRATION FOR YOUR BATHROOM

- Colorful, loud pieces with a lot of personality for your water closet
- A gallery wall of nudes, both photography and sketches
- A large piece above your tub to create a statement area
- Place a piece in the reflection of the mirror so that it can be seen from multiple angles.
- Artist Angela Chrusciaki Blehm placed a wood painting in one of her bathrooms with the perfect contrasting wall. The sculptural piece does well with the occasional steam and can be cleaned when necessary. The stronger material will hold well over time with any moisture, making it a great candidate for a bathroom.

Opposite: Artwork and design by Angela Chrusciaki Blehm. Photo by Justin Salem Meyer. Background artwork by Theodora Miller.

Artwork by Angela Chrusciaki Blehm, Elsie Larson, Allison James, Fares Micue, Ella Richards, Betsy Enzensberger, Kristi Kohut, and Kim Eubank.

INSPIRATION FOR

all other rooms

Living Room

The living room is your place to shine: Almost anything goes. Your artwork can showcase how you want the room to feel and be a conversation piece.

If you are planning a classic look of a gorgeous piece above a fireplace, give the mantel a feel while a fire is burning to test how much heat is omitted. If the wall is warm in any way, you'll want to plan accordingly with your work of art and choose a material that can withstand a little heat.

Stairwell

This client's grand entry and stairwell show off what works well in this type of space. Stairwells can be excellent locations for meaningful pieces, such as children's artwork or personal family photos. Often stairwells are less public-facing areas, so personal artwork and décor work well.

This client chose a refined color palette to help connect the artwork, as well as a subject matter mix of figural work with abstracts. Stairwells can be such confined spaces, a "connective tissue" and limited color palette helps to keep the eye moving and keep it from feeling overwhelming.

Artwork by Gina Julian, Hillary Howorth, Keavy Murphree, Klein Reid, Beau Jones, Rolando Rosler, Gregory Block, and Helle Mardahl. Design by Gina Julian. Photo by Shannon Fontaine.

Wolf Kahn
THE 21ST CENTURY ART BOOK
FRANK STELLA
MOOD
ANNE HEPFER
Joan Mitchell
A PORTRAIT OF BOWIE

Dining Room

The dining room is one of my favorite places to design within a theme. Here you can see my own kitchen and dining room. The dining space has been covered in a stunning wallpaper mural and the artwork has been chosen to follow the outdoor landscape theme with florals and a Hunt Slonem bunny.

This can also be a place where you choose to bring the drama. That can mean moodier pieces with deeper or more dramatic colorways or bold pairings. It can create a more intimate or romantic setting with those bolder colors.

Opposite: Artwork by Hunt Slonem and Jenna Brownlee.

Opposite: Artwork by Katie Craig and collected vintage pieces. *Above:* Artwork by Shannon Coppage. Design by Mallory Mathison Interiors. Photo Jeff Herr Photo.

Kids' Bedrooms

It's recommended that you do not place a work of art that is heavy over a crib or changing table. Items that are plush, soft, or lightweight are your goal if you have a large wall above these areas.

For a child's room I like to think about long-term pieces that can grow with the child over time. Inexpensive prints are a great way to start as the child's room décor will most likely change many times throughout the years. Replacing these with nicer pieces one by one will help them build a collection early!

Think playful, fun, and inspiring. Framing with bright, bold colors can take artwork into fun mode for a kid's bedroom. As they grow, just changing out the framing can help the piece become more sophisticated as the child grows!

Opposite: Artwork by Jose Romussi, Angela Chrusciaki Blehm, Kristi Kohut, and Betsy Enzensberger. Giraffe made by Robert Lidgett. *Left:* Artwork by Angela Chrusciaki Blehm.

DISPLAYING ARTWORK BY EMERGING ARTISTS

(AKA, YOUR KIDS)

If you have young artists in your life, you may be receiving a lot of artwork each week and need a solution (or two) to display their creations. I believe we can go beyond the classic magnet-on-the-fridge technique. I have a designated location for display, which has helped the dreaded "what did you do with my artwork?" conversation with my budding artist. If you want to show your love for both the creator and the artwork, but also want to do so in a design-friendly manner, here are some clever tricks.

1. Go old school with a giant corkboard. Having a single, contained display area can help focus the visual weight of all that artwork. It feels fun, chaotic, and colorful—just the way kids' art should feel.

2. Use two eye hooks and picture-hanging wire to create a taut line. Then use binder clips to hang artwork on the wire so that each piece can be displayed and easily replaced without harming your wall or paint job.

3. Hang empty vintage frames in a gallery wall style. Artwork can be taped onto the wall inside of each frame. It makes each piece feel special and can be easily changed out after each piece has received its due attention.

4. For the pieces that you want to display forever, scan and upload them to an online printing site and have them printed at a large scale with a frame to make it feel more finished. You can also combine multiple pieces at a smaller scale to display more than one without running out of room.

5. For one of my favorite projects, I gave my children a framed canvas that I had found at a charity thrift store. Then I let them go wild, and they created a large piece that goes beautifully in our home *and* displays their creativity.

PRO TIP: Give them only colors that match your home and color palette.

AN ARTFUL CONVERSATION WITH

GINA JULIAN

Gina Julian was born and raised in Nashville, Tennessee. With more than twenty years of art direction, publishing, and web development experience under her belt, she now enjoys painting full-time from her studio in Nolensville, Tennessee. She has a love of interior design and wholeheartedly believes in the positive impact of living with art and experiencing it on a daily basis.

LIZ: As an artist, how do you decide which artwork and artists you would like to collect?

GINA: I've always collected art that either made me happy or that totally freaks me out. I've never purchased a piece of art simply because of who the artist is. I have to really love the art and want to live with it. Price point is also a consideration, and when I find an artist or a piece of art that I absolutely love, I will save up my money as long as it takes to get it. Because I'm an artist myself, I tend to prioritize art purchases over other things like trendy clothing, bags, jewelry, etc. After all, it makes my home way more interesting and it lasts a lot longer than fashion trends!

LIZ: How do you decide if a piece is "the one" for you?

GINA: There are so many reasons that I want to live with a piece of art. This is a short list of them, and the more boxes that get checked, the more I know it's "the one." These reasons might include:

- I want it to be bright and cheerful.
- I want it to evoke happy memories.
- I want it to capture the attention of my guests and make them happy.
- I want it to speak to others about my preferences and my past.
- I want others to know that I like weird stuff and I have a wicked sense of humor.
- I want to laugh and make others laugh.
- I want to sit in awe and wonder and think "how did the artist do that?!?!"

LIZ: **Do you have any specific ways you love to install? Any fun and out-of-the-box ideas?**

GINA: Because I have so much art, I've started using a picture rail hanging system in my home wherever possible. I prefer the kind with clear Perlon cords, but you can also use brass hangers that hook onto a picture rail for a more traditional look. I have a lighted standing brass easel that is great for filling an empty corner of a room, and smaller ones for layering art on a tabletop. I have a salon-style gallery wall in my TV room that is filled with lots of small pieces of art and a few larger paintings. Nothing matches and it's a big hodgepodge that makes me happy. I display glass art on my coffee table and have art tucked into my bookshelves. And while I haven't done this yet in my own home, I also really love the look of hanging art on the front of shelving that is packed to the brim with books, and I love the idea of hanging art in front of a mirror or a window (only if the back is sealed and protected from sunlight). Last but not least, I would love to have a diorama installed into a wall or column in my home. I think it would be the ultimate quirky, fun thing for my guests to discover!

LIZ: **Do you have a theme or connecting idea with your collection?**

GINA: I collect a lot of art that features food, specifically colorful sweet treats. I had issues with food as a child and I was given sweets to comfort or as a reward, and so I think this is my way of having it in my life as an adult, but in a much healthier way. I also have a penchant for surrealism, and this is where I can really let my freak flag fly. I love art that makes you take a second look to figure out what's really going on.

LIZ: **Do you have a favorite story about any of the pieces you own?**

GINA: I collected a painting that is one of my favorites because of the beauty and the interaction with the artist and his gallery. Tjalf Sparnaay is a Dutch photorealist painter, and I was in love with his style. A commission was out of my price point, but later I saw he was making smaller works for a gallery show in New York. I spoke to the gallery and found the perfect piece, but didn't know if I could afford it. The gallerist told me "make me an offer!" I made a fair offer and it was accepted! I emailed Tjalf and he immediately responded thanking me and sent me photos of the piece while it was being painted.

Background artwork by Jennifer Allevato.

THE ALL-IMPORTANT

Zoom background

The pandemic and 2020 changed the world in so many ways, including making it necessary for many people to have a spot in their home or office (or both) to take video meetings. Finding the perfect piece of art to sit in front of has become an art in and of itself. There are now full Reddit threads about Zoom backgrounds—it's become ubiquitous. My tips include the following:

- Find an artwork that fills the space. I have been on many a video call with one tiny diploma nailed off to the side. We can do better!
- Choose an abstract piece. I personally think that the role of a work of art in your office is to be beautiful but not distracting. An abstract work eliminates the issue of your meeting attendees trying to figure out what your artwork depicts instead of paying attention to what you are saying.
- Don't choose a family photo. These, too, are distracting and can look like people are peeking over your shoulder. How about that visual?
- Nothing offensive or controversial. This rule may be controversial itself, but I think this includes sports teams too. I won't call out which team, but I have truly thought, "Oh man, they root for the rival team," while on business calls. Did it change the outcome of the meeting? No. Did I think a little less of them? Just a tiny bit. I love sports and the teams I root for are in my DNA, but art is supposed to show off your personality, not just your interests—even if those interests are intense. There are exceptions, but unless you're the president of baseball operations for the Dodgers, that framed poster of Shohei Ohtani doesn't need to be over your shoulder for every business call.
- Think warm, minimal, and abstract, and you'll find the perfect Zoom background.

Opposite: Artwork by Gina Julian, Brian Burt, Nick Rhodes, Alan LeQuire, Tjalf Sparnaay, Cathy Lancaster, Blair Wheeler, and Helle Mardahl. Design by Gina Julian. Photo by Shannon Fontaine.

Lotus
CAKE MIX BIBLE
GEM
Virgil Abloh™ ICONS
CHIC STAYS
PRADA
LOUIS VUITTON
Dior
love
DIOR IN BLOOM
DIGITAL PHOTOGRAPHY
SLATE
IBIZA
ROCK
INSIDE
DECORATE
HOCKNEY

WONDERLAND SUMMER THORNTON
GLAMOROUS ROOMS JAN SHOWERS
Roar!
DEMSEY BEHIND THE BLUE DOOR
ROTHKO

WHAT ABOUT

sculpture?

Yes, what about sculpture? For this book, we are focusing primarily on the artwork styles and mediums that are hung on the wall either by canvas or frame. Adding sculpture to your home adds an additional layer for a more curated look. Sculptural elements are also a great way to add unexpected artful elements throughout your home, such as sculptural flowers in a vase instead of natural flowers.

Here are some ideas for incorporating and displaying sculpture throughout any space.

A PEDESTAL elevates sculptures to create a museum-worthy display. Choose a pedestal in marble, acrylic, or wood to complement the piece and add some warmth.

A BUILT-IN NICHE allows accent lighting for a site-specific and sophisticated focal point. Similarly, a floating shelf allows for interesting displays with smaller sculptures that can be paired in vignettes with other décor items like books or related objects.

FLOOR PLACEMENT FOR LARGER PIECES works well in corners, next to fireplaces, or near windows to frame a view. For these larger pieces, it's extra important to think about how you use a space and to make sure the sculpture does not create a pinch-point in a walking path.

A GLASS OR ACRYLIC CASE can be appropriate for smaller or more delicate sculptures while maintaining visibility of the piece.

COFFEE TABLES, SOFA TABLES, AND BOOKSHELVES are also excellent locations for smaller sculpture. This incorporates the art into furniture and placements that already exist around your home, so the flow is seamless.

Opposite: Artwork by Lindsey Kelley, Madison Summerlin, Serge Zelikson, Terry Wright, Ashley Treece, and Susannah Carson. Design by Andrea Brooks Interiors. Photo by Mark Jackson / CHROMA.

A CEILING MOBILE OR HANGING SCULPTURE offers the ability to think about a "fifth wall" in your room. Using that negative space helps free up walls and other surfaces and keeps your artwork up and out of the way, but also aids your eye in moving around the room.

You'll want to make sure that larger pieces are still sitting eye level, or close to, just as you would with any other piece. This can mean you'll need to adjust the pedestal so that piece sits higher or lower. Additionally, you can also sit a smaller pedestal on a piece of furniture or bookshelf for that coveted layered look.

Many of the important considerations when purchasing or commissioning sculpture are the same as when you are purchasing other types of art. Size and scale become a key factor to ensure the piece fits proportionally within the intended space and interacts with your space and furniture. Taking a sculpture home from a gallery or studio space and incorporating it into a living space is making a transition between two very different environments. Placement and safety also become a larger consideration as sculpture, depending on the material, can weigh quite a bit. Materials like marble, stone, or wood can injure a person or pet if an accident happens. You'll want to ensure stability and even consider wall-mounting or floor-mounting options for added security. Finally, both natural and artificial lighting can affect how the sculpture looks throughout the day. Sculpture has a tendency to create larger shadows when not lit well enough or incorrectly. We've spoken of hidden costs as well, and shipping and installation are additional budget items to consider when you are purchasing sculpture.

Outdoor sculpture is also an option with its own set of things to consider. Material durability is important to consider depending on your climate. If you live in a climate that experiences all four seasons, weather-resistant materials will be even more important for you to think about. Bronze, stainless steel, and corten steel are all common materials for outdoor sculpture and they are resistant to rust and aging. Stone and concrete can be both classic and durable and can withstand the elements. If you are considering a sculpture that has materials like glass or wood, ask the artist if they have been sealed or treated and what types of maintenance are required through the years.

Artwork by Michelle Armas. Design by Cara Fineman, DAG Design.
Photo by Sarah Winchester Studios.

I have worked with clients who have large sculptures made in durable materials, but they have needed the sculptures repainted after years outside during Iowa winters. When you are purchasing the artwork, ask the artist what the process will be if restoration is needed in the coming years. This can include the exact maintenance notes and even the paint color and type if there is any color included in the piece. Keeping these notes will save you a lot of work down the line. Take it from my experience of trying to track down artists and jogging their memories about pieces they created thirty years prior. You don't want to be in that situation.

Additionally, with outdoor sculpture, large pieces will often require a concrete or stone base. A simple base will help keep the sculpture from sinking into soft ground, protect it from some weather elements, and prevent early deterioration. The base must be heavy enough to prevent tipping, especially in any windy conditions or where a person may attempt to climb it. The sculpture's center of gravity should be balanced on the base, and you should consider bolting or welding the piece for extra security. Concrete footings may also be needed for large sculptures, especially in soft soil. Hidden fasteners or underground supports can be a theft prevention strategy if that is also needed. The not-so-sexy part of outdoor sculpture placement is also thinking about drainage. You'll need to prevent water pooling on the base, which can damage materials and cause instability. You can design a base with sloped edges or subtle drainage holes to prevent moisture damage. Simply checking on your piece regularly by knocking off snow or debris can help add years to the life of materials.

If you want to incorporate a sculpture into your landscaping, think of your outdoor space as you would your interior home. Consider positioning your sculptures to frame a landscape view or to draw your eye toward a natural element, like a garden patch or tree line. Hanging or suspended sculptures can use wind-activated kinetic elements to add movement. Placing the sculptures at the end of a pathway or within a flower bed adds a beautiful visual element and creates a great contrast to the natural landscape.

OKAY, AND WHAT ABOUT

digital work?

Digital artwork is here to stay and can add a really special and different element to your collection. These video- or image-based pieces can offer dynamic, customizable, and interactive elements that traditional media cannot. Historically, one of the issues with digital artwork is how to display the piece when technology becomes outdated over time. Some original digital pieces created by artists are on VHS tapes—how many people still have those laying around the house?

Digital pieces are becoming more mainstream and there are now screens created specifically for the display of electronic-based pieces. They can be displayed on your phone's home screen so you carry your artwork around with you wherever you go.

HERE'S HOW YOU CAN INTEGRATE DIGITAL ART INTO YOUR SPACE

DIGITAL FRAMES are high-resolution screens that allow for seamless rotation and static displays. These frames allow for the storage of multiple pieces, so if you have limited wall space, this can be an excellent option.

PROJECTION MAPPING is where a projector is installed, usually from the ceiling, and you are able to transform your blank wall into a digital canvas. This is most commonly used in museums that have a video projection room where viewers can enter into a darkened space to enjoy a piece. A version of this can also be created with a strong projector.

AUGMENTED REALITY AND VIRTUAL REALITY, where collectors can create a virtual gallery or interactive space they can "walk" through or enjoy, are now also options.

Ownership and authenticity have become hotbed discussion topics when it comes to digital artwork. Earlier, I defined NFT (non-fungible token), but let's dive a bit deeper into the topic to understand how someone can own an NFT that seemingly feels like it can be replicated. Each NFT uses blockchain technology to show the provenance (history of ownership) through a digital certificate. This imprint shows who the owner is. A common question is, "What if someone takes a screenshot of my digital art/NFT?" Well, they may have a screenshot like someone may own a poster of the *Mona Lisa*, but only the Louvre owns the true masterpiece.

Over the years, I have done my best to stay away from questions on whether or not NFTs in particular are here to stay and if they will continue to hold their value. There's a famous video clip from 1994 of Katie Couric and Bryant Gumbel wondering, "What is the Internet anyway?" At the time, it was something new, foreign, and hard to understand, but today it is incredibly commonplace. In a good-natured way, it's funny—How could they not understand the internet? NFTs feel the same to a lot of people. Plus, we have already seen the prices of NFTs go on a roller-coaster ride, so the financial investment is very risky. At the time of this printing, I understand what NFTs are, why they are attractive to some people, and how they work. All that considered, they are still not something I will personally be collecting. I love the satisfaction that comes with hanging a physical piece on the wall. The majority of my clients are this way too and NFTs have been, historically, looked at as an investment using artwork. I am currently summing them up as "good for them, not for me." But who knows, someone someday may pull this quote to show how much has changed over time.

There are a few different ways to show ownership of a digital piece. The first being the blockchain authorization technology from an NFT. Additionally, artists create limited editions of work so that a design is not creating an infinitely reproducible file. Finally, you may also receive a smart contract, which is when a digital work comes with built-in resale rights for an artist. This means that the artist will receive some sort of commission or compensation for future sales if the piece is sold at auction. This is to prevent cases where an artwork is originally sold for a low retail price, and after years of appreciation in value the artwork is sold for millions of dollars. This has happened many times. Without resell rights (or a droit de suite) the artist would not see any compensation for that increase in value. The additional funds would all go to the buyer, who, of course, did not create the piece.

Two other things to consider when purchasing NFT artwork are, first, making sure you have multiple copies in high-resolution formats on external hard drives or cloud storage. These formats can include TIFF, PNG, and MP4 for video. This will ensure that no matter the technology, you will be able to view your digital piece. And second, problem solving for the long-term accessibility of your piece is something to think about in the beginning. If you have access to the artist or the originating gallery, ask how you can display the digital piece in perpetuity, even if the technology needs change. The hope here is to always display artwork in accordance with the artist's original intentions. Are there certain formats that are off-limits? Any technology that will or will not work? Has the artist thought about how the piece remains in perpetuity?

Although both sculpture and digital works require different considerations than more typical canvases and framed work, many things remain constant. Get proper information about care, maintenance, and display upfront, and they can be beautiful additions to your collection.

Above: Artwork by Rebecca Stern. Design by Meghan Blum Interiors. Photo by Brooke Pavel.

This page: Artwork collected vintage pieces. Design and photo by Kate Pearce Vintage. *Opposite:* Background artwork by Christina Flowers.

CHAPTER

Gallery Walls

WILL NEVER GO OUT OF STYLE

SIX

Gallery walls are one of my favorite things to create because buying smaller works by a variety of artists over time is a wonderful way to collect. A gallery wall can truly tell a story of a person or family and it is the perfect way to add a personal touch to your home. All of this is to say, they can be a reflection of the individual or family. Each one is different based on the artwork that has been collected, the space it is covering, and the design elements working together. This is your chance to be creative. Think of a collection that goes up and over windows or around a door. Think artwork that has been collected over years or decades. Think starting small and making it larger over time!

One of the best things about a gallery wall is that it can grow as you collect and looks good at all different stages. The downside is that, if not done properly, it can look cluttered. It truly is an art, not a science, when putting together a collection. Follow the tips below and you will nail it every time. (Pun intended, of course.)

This page: Background artwork by Jennifer Allevato. *Opposite:* Artwork, design, and photo by Scout Design Studio.

Collecting Tips

1. Collect a variety of sizes.

A variance in size is one of the best ways to keep the gallery wall from looking cluttered. Having larger central pieces will give the gallery wall a focal point that everything "radiates" out from.

2. Collect a variety of mediums.

Collecting a variety of mediums is an amazing way to keep your gallery wall from looking too flat or one-dimensional. We want the wall to look collected. Consider mixed media pieces that use string or pottery. Consider vintage pieces like beautiful plates or copper pieces. Consider any wall-hanging sculpture. Throw in a family photo or two.

3. Collect artworks that have "connective tissue."

To continue with the cohesion in the artwork, my general rule is for about half of the pieces to have some sort of connective tissue. This connection can be the same artist, the same accent color carried throughout each piece, or even the same topic or style. I love this example of a collection found on Facebook Marketplace of vintage sea captains displayed throughout the hallway of a seaside home.

4. Frame your collection in three frame styles or less.

Framing your collection in a cohesive way makes the entire wall feel intentional. The artwork can have so many different styles but if the frames are similar it will look as though you thought through every purchase. I often like to decide between a wood tone or black and then choose two styles in that colorway. The third frame style I like to add in as an accent is a metallic frame. I do fewer of these, but they add the perfect touch of glimmer and interest to the wall.

Opposite: Artwork are vintage collected pieces. Design and photo by Susan Quinlan Ripke. Background artwork by Daisy Faith.

Hanging Tips

1. Start with the largest piece first.

The largest piece is your focal spot. With any gallery wall, we want to keep our eyes moving throughout the space. The large piece near the center will give your eye the first place to go. Then the pieces with the connective tissue act as a roadmap to keep your eyes moving to see everything.

2. Keep your spacing as consistent as possible.

This is a goal more than a rule. The general rule of thumb says to keep artwork between three inches and ten inches apart. Choose a distance, such as five inches, and keep that distance throughout the gallery wall. Any less than three inches and the artwork feels too close and messy. Any farther apart than ten inches and the artwork doesn't feel connected. When you are working with multiple sizes and shapes, this is not always possible, but consistency is key when working on a gallery wall.

3. Choose odd numbers for your clusters.

A design rule is to always choose odd numbers of elements to make a design or composition more aesthetically pleasing. I think our eyes like an odd number best because there is always a centered piece this way. The Rule of Odds works whether you are working with three pieces or more than twenty going up a stairwell.

4. Lay the gallery wall on the floor first to make your map.

Find a space in your home with room to spread out, and lay the artwork on the floor. This is the easiest way possible to play with different arrangements without doing damage to your wall. Too many times, I have seen people start putting nails in the wall without a plan and—you guessed it!—it just doesn't work.

5. Create a template out of craft paper.

Another great way to prep your gallery wall is by tracing the artwork onto paper and cutting out the shapes. You can then use painter's tape to keep the template in place on the wall. This is the best way to understand how the artwork will take up space on the wall. Measure the distance between the top of the artwork and the wire when taut. Then measure that distance and make a mark on the template. This is the foolproof way to get your nails in the perfect spot.

6. Balance is key.

The largest piece does not have to be in the center, but do make sure that your composition is overall balanced in terms of "visual weight." You can create asymmetrical or symmetrical balance as long as the pieces visually take up the same amount of space. For example, three pieces may take up the same amount of visual space as one large piece.

Artwork by Monica Ajenjo, Paige Ledom, Jose Romussi, AK Hardeman, and collected vintage pieces.

LOUVRE

OTHER THINGS TO

keep in mind

1. Think linear.

Another option is to keep the frames the exact same size and type. This is where you can have fun and play with things like mat size, negative space, and repetition. Think of compositions: three or five pieces across, or three rows of three pieces to create a large square. Even though this design is more uniform, there are still plenty of ways to be creative. Another idea would be to have a series of similar pieces using an unusual centerpiece that offsets the otherwise uniform look of the gallery wall. When hanging art, I love when you can create something unexpected like one piece that strays from the pattern. When you are playing with linear designs, though, precision is key. Your eye will notice when something is not level or uneven. Get that measuring tape and level out and get ready to be exact!

2. Bring in non-art items.

Including a mirror in a gallery wall is a go-to trick for many designers. It helps make the room look larger through the reflection and can have an interesting shape. I also encourage you to think about other special mementos that you have collected over the years. For example, I held on to my license plate from when I lived in California. When it was time to create a gallery wall for my son, it added the right amount of texture and grit to the space.

3. Put it on a shelf!

Using picture shelves is a favorite way to create a location that can change easily without leaving damage behind. For years, I used a long gallery wall shelf in our living room. I changed out certain pieces seasonally and it was also easy for me to add in new favorite photos as our family grew. This is a great alternative for those of us who get bored easily with décor. Just by playing with the composition and display, you can make a wall feel entirely different in a few minutes. Again, a variety of sizes here will help lead the eye throughout the collection and will make the arrangement feel more organic. Layering the pieces just a bit makes the display feel a little more casual and welcoming as well. Who doesn't love a low-budget makeover?

Opposite: Artwork by Tina Ehrlich, Eliana Bernard, and Betsy Enzensberger.

LET'S DISSECT WHY THESE

gallery walls

WORK

An example straight from the walls of my gallery. Here you can see we have the work of nine different artists on one large wall. Here's why it works:

- Cohesive colors are carried throughout the wall. Blues and greens are pulled from the large AK Hardeman floral abstract piece down the wall in multiple pieces.
- There is cohesion in subject matter with three floral pieces that are equal distances apart. Your eye naturally looks for similar items and this helps carry your attention throughout the entire wall. Additionally, there are two figural pieces and four abstract pieces.
- There is balance in the design based on the visual weight being heavy on either end with a pattern created in the center 1-2-1-2 installation.

Artwork by AK Hardeman, Brittany Atkinson, Kate Blomquist, Marcy Cook Vreeland, Jaime McCarrier, Alexandra Ackerman, Andrea Ferrigno, Jenna Brownlee, and Makiko Harris.

- This gallery wall uses a variety of mediums and sculptural elements. The wall shelves painted the same colors as the walls create an illusion that the collected objects are very much a part of the gallery wall. This creates wonderful visual interest by bringing in metals, wood, glass, and organic materials.
- The tonal blues in the artwork pair well together and also blend well with the wall colors. This is a great example of wall color playing with artwork and adding to the overall aesthetic conversation.
- There are a variety of mediums, styles, and sizes to keep the viewer looking at all the pieces displayed.

- This gallery wall feels fun, eclectic, and built over time. The pennant and flag on either end of the wall help play with the visual balance and make your eye leap to either side.
- The wall wraps around the edge and visually includes the hanging globe.
- There are three types of framing—black, gold, and silver. All three are neutrals and play well with the color story throughout the room.
- Have you heard of the "rule of unexpected red"? It works both in interior design and in your clothing. The rule states that a pop of red basically always works and feels sophisticated. The pops of red in the artwork help connect the design with the stadium chairs and red shelf.

Above: Artwork collected vintage pieces, with a print by The Red Door Press. *Opposite:* Artwork by Allison James, Liz Lidgett, Kate Blomquist, and Gina Julian.

- This gallery wall in the home of artist Gina Julian is an excellent example of including unexpected shapes. Using the same square or rectangle repeatedly can start to feel too uniform. When you intersperse a variety of interesting shapes as Gina did here, it becomes a visual feast that your eyes want to devour. The deep navy wall helps all the bright and bold pieces pop, and she has kept to simple metallic frames to showcase the art. She has created variety in the pieces while staying refined in the framing.

Above: Artwork by Dorna May, Cat Seyler, Hanna Lane, Andres Bustamante, Josh Crow, Brandon Bird, Blair Wheeler, Francesco Lo Castro, Mallory Page, Suzy Lindow, Marcelo Suaznabar, Julia Martin, Carey Haynes, Hailey Welker, Megan Coonelly, Joel Penkman, Alexis Walter, Trevor Mikula, and Annie Wildey. Design by Gina Julian. Photo by Shannon Fontaine. *Opposite:* Artwork by Bethany Mabee and Anna Beurskens, with collected vintage pieces. Design by Jordan Leigh Woodward. Photo by Kaitlin Green.

- TVs have long been the bane of many a designer's existence. Visually, they create a black hole in an otherwise lovely room. Here, designer Jordan Leigh Woodard has displayed a collection of art and found objects around the television that both distracts from the television and complements it with the black accents. The clock and paddle add utilitarian objects into the gallery wall, but the artwork and their color add warmth, using earthy tones.
- Of course, there is also the invention of the art TV where different images can be displayed while the television is asleep or not being watched. This then gives an opportunity to use the television as just one piece of a larger gallery wall. With frames being added now to the edges of the television, they can become so well disguised that they look like an intentional piece of artwork.

Top: Artwork by Amanda McLaurin. Design by Katie Massop. *Bottom:* Artwork and design by Angela Chrusciaki Blehm. Photo by Justin Salem Meyer.

GALLERY WALL TIPS FOR

renters

All of these nails in the drywall are all well and good if you own your home, but what should renters do? As a renter, I always favored the "ask for forgiveness later" method; however, I know that's not great advice. The true answer is that you need to be creative with your display, but the no-holes-in-your-rental-walls rule doesn't exclude you from owning and living with beautiful artwork.

- Your fail-safe, easiest, and dare I say most stylish way to display artwork without nails is the classic lean. The main way to get this one right is to have one large piece as your visual anchor. If you have room above a dresser, I would go large with a framed 30 x 40-inch piece or larger. Use the design rule of using odd numbers and make sure each piece has a different size, so that the styling feels organic.
- Hang your artwork on your furniture. Of course, this works better for the IKEA variety than a family heirloom, but a painting on a bookshelf, either leaned or hanging from a nail hook, is a great look. Painted furniture, like a wall, can be patched if you are worried about the mark left behind.
- A large easel is not just for artists. Using a wooden or clear acrylic easel can act as a room divider, if needed, or the perfect way to display a larger piece against a wall backdrop. I love to collect tabletop easels; some have a lighting system attached, so they work as a table lamp and ambience as well as a display for your artwork.
- Controversial as it may be, I love the look of a piece of artwork on a door. If you have a coat hook attached to a door, then, in my mind, you have an art-hanging hook on your door. Add a beautiful ribbon to the back of the artwork, looped through the wire or hanger, and create a bow at the top to hang from the door hook.
- Above my own bed at home, I have used that same bow technique to hang a lightweight vintage piece from a window curtain rod.

Look beyond just your walls as a renter and you will start to see that the possibilities are endless. More traditional rent-friendly options like 3M strips and washi tape are also excellent options for more lightweight artwork.

This page: Artwork by Jennifer Allevato. *Opposite:* Background artwork by Christina Flowers.

CHAPTER

Install, DISPLAY, AND PRESERVE

THE GUIDE TO GETTING IT RIGHT

SEVEN

I don't mean to oversell it, but this is the chapter that will help solve many a marital squabble. The number one thing I hear from clients about installing art: "My spouse and I can't agree on how to hang the art." I hear "My spouse is very tall and so they hang their art tall too!" I hear "We don't know how to hang the art so we just keep it on the ground waiting for one of us to do it." And I hear "I am too scared to make a hole in my wall because I am going to make a mistake." Basically, I hear it all. If you can personally identify with any of those statements, please use this chapter as your ultimate art-hanging guidebook. Come back to it again and again when you have questions about how high an artwork should be or how far apart. Artwork, of course, is meant to be enjoyed and you can only do that if you feel confident enough to hang the piece and put the damn hole in the wall.

This page: Background artwork by Kristen Abbott. *Opposite:* Artwork by Elisa Sheehan. Design by Betsy Olmsted. Photo by Elizabeth Haynes Photography.

Artwork by Jennifer Allevato.

FIRST THINGS FIRST.

how do I install

AN ARTWORK?

TOOLS

Tape measure: *I prefer one that is a little more heavy duty so it doesn't droop!*

Hammer

Pencil

Level: *I like a small level that I can carry anywhere, but most days an app on your phone will do the trick too!*

Nail: If your artwork has a wire on the back, you'll want to use an art hanging hook. Check the weight that the hook is approved for! If it's a long, wide piece, you'll need more than one.

MEASUREMENTS

Here is the hard and fast rule: If you are hanging a single piece of artwork on a wall with no furniture below it, the center of that piece should be 60 inches from the ground. Because the average eye level is between 58 and 60 inches, this rule is followed regardless of the height of the wall or the piece. It does not change if the people who live in the home are tall or short. We work under the assumption that other humans may enter your home who do not live there. Even if you're antisocial, this is still the rule. (Can you tell I am trying to solve any and all arguments?)

Here's how the math goes: Let's say an artwork is 30 × 30 inches. (This means that the piece is 30 inches tall.) You divide the height of the piece in half and add that number to 60 inches. For this piece you would add 15 to 60 and end up with 75. This is now the height that the top of our piece should be. Look at the back of the piece: How does it hang? If there is a wire, measure the distance between the wire (while taut) and the top of the piece. Let's say that distance is 10 inches. That means the nail will go into the wall at 65 inches from the ground.

If we were writing this out like a math equation and we needed to show our work, this is how it would look.

(Height of the piece / divided by 2) + 60 - the distance between the wire and top of the piece = where the nail goes into the wall.

This is the same rule whether the back of the piece is a wire, a claw hanger, or D rings. Large pieces of artwork often do not have a wire, but do have a D ring screwed into the back on both sides of the piece. These can be tricky to get level because they allow for less wiggle room, but follow the steps and you'll be successful.

The above steps are for a totally blank wall. I'll address the math for hanging art above furniture on page 188.

If you are hanging multiple pieces, for example in a vertical row of three or a large gallery wall, the center of ALL the work should be 60 inches above the floor. Let's take our vertical row of three example.

Let's say each piece is 20 x 20 inches and you'd like 3 inches between each piece. Your math equation would look like this:

(20 × 3) + (3 × 2) = 66 inches (66 / 2) + 60 = 93 inches

This means that the top piece should be at 93 inches above the floor. Hang the top piece first. Measure 3 inches from the bottom of the piece, and then measure the distance for the next piece from the wire. 3 + that number will give you the answer for where the next nail goes, and so on.

For a gallery wall, I'd recommend first laying out the design on the floor showing your distances between each piece and the arrangement you'd like. Measure the entire design to find the height and you'll find the center of the arrangement. Finding the center of the design will be your north star no matter what you are hanging.

Opposite: Artwork by Jennifer Allevato.

INSTALLING ARTWORK ON A BLANK WALL

1

2

3

4

5

STEP 1: Find the center of the area where you would like to hang your artwork. This may be a full wall or it may be the center of a piece of furniture, or the open area between two pieces of furniture. Make a faint line with your pencil once you have found center.

STEP 2: Find the solution for your formula. Again: (Height of the piece / divided by 2) + 60 inches - the distance between the wire and top of the piece = where the nail goes into the wall.

Use your pencil to mark an x. If it is a long piece horizontally, I often will create two x's centered on the center point. Depending on how long the piece is, they can be 12 to 36 inches (or more) apart. Long horizontal pieces have a tendency to become askew easily. Two hooks can help prevent the piece from becoming uneven.

STEP 3: It's time to put a hole in the wall! Place your hook and nail in the wall with your hammer.

STEP 4: Hang the piece!

STEP 5: Use your level and enjoy your freshly hung artwork!

WHERE TO

hang art

Stairs

If you are hanging an artwork or multiple artworks on the stairs, the math is a little different. You apply the eyeline rule of 60 inches to each individual stair. If it feels easier, a good rule of thumb is to measure 4 feet up from the stair tread you are hanging your artwork above: The 4-feet mark is the measurement for the bottom of the frame. This means that when you measure the distance for the wire, you will be measuring from the bottom of the frame instead. Your math equation would look like this:

Distance from bottom of artwork to top of wire + 48 = distance from tread where the nail should be hung. If there is a railing, you want the bottom of your piece to have at least 6 inches' distance at the center of the piece.

Above Furniture

If you are hanging an artwork above a piece of furniture, most often our original equation stays the same. However, because we are adding an additional visual element, we need to take in the entire vignette and how each item works together as a whole. The bottom edge of your artwork should be 12 inches above a piece of furniture, which means you may have to make your eyeline higher. That distance will allow space so heads don't knock the artwork if it's above a sofa, or clear items on a table. Once you have done the math equation, if the bottom of the piece is lower than the furniture you can adjust by adding 10 + the distance below the furniture to your final number.

Opposite: Artwork and design by Gina Julian. Photo by Shannon Fontaine.

S IS FOR STYLE
JOHN DERIAN
ANNIE LEIBOVITZ
DAVID BOWIE ICON
BUTTERFLIES
Hunt Slonem

HOW TO INSTALL ARTWORK ABOVE FURNITURE

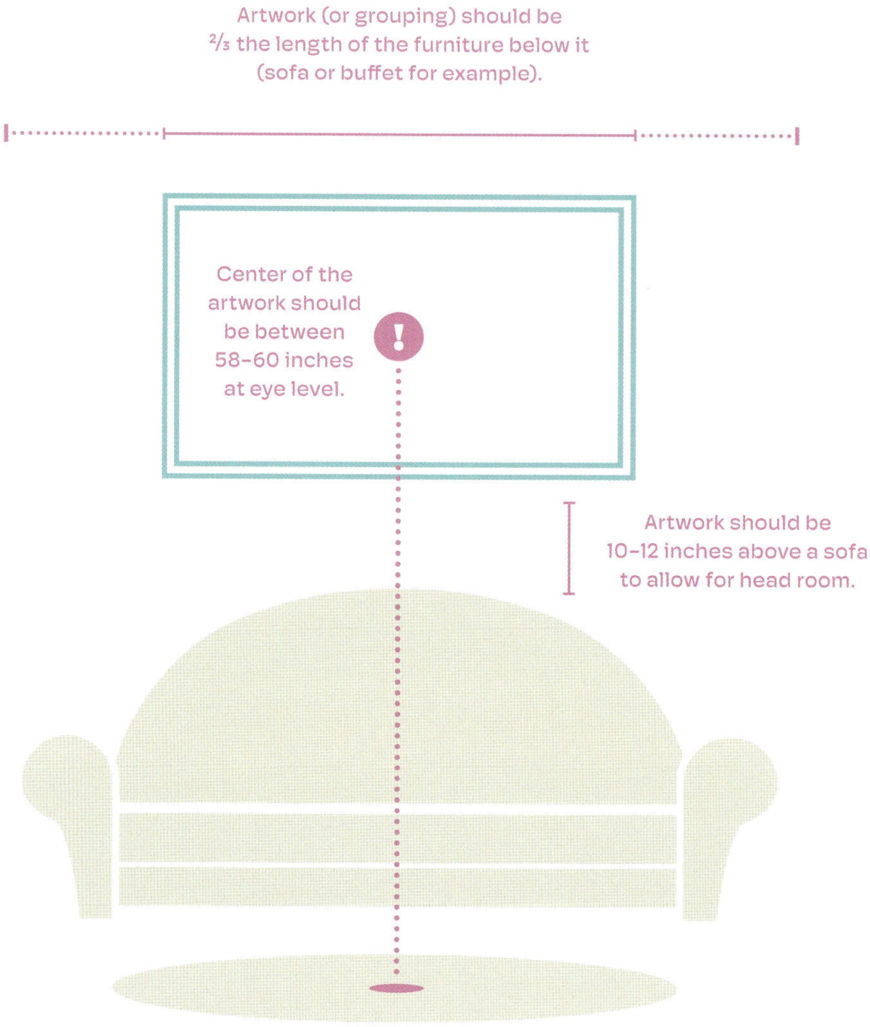

Artwork (or grouping) should be ⅔ the length of the furniture below it (sofa or buffet for example).

Center of the artwork should be between 58–60 inches at eye level.

Artwork should be 10–12 inches above a sofa to allow for head room.

STEP 1: The center of your artwork should be at eye level.

STEP 2: Measure the artwork height and divide by 2. Add one half of the artwork height to the eye level of your artwork. This is the top of your artwork.

STEP 3: Pull the wire on the back of the piece tight and measure the distance between the wire and the top of the piece. Make a small mark. This is where your hook goes.

STEP 4: Hang the artwork and adore your walls!

Play with Scale

Playing with size and scale can be one of the best ways to have great impact with artwork and interior design relatively easily. This is also where I tell you to go ahead and forget all the rules I just told you about the size of a piece needed.

If you want to go extra-large, find an oversize statement piece that will anchor the room and serve as a focal point, drawing attention and setting the tone for the space. Additionally, a dramatically oversized piece in a smaller room can make the space feel grander.

Using a smaller piece is not only often more friendly to your wallet, but it gives you the opportunity to place artwork in some of those fun, unexpected places. It also gives you the chance to play with negative space or, as I like to call it, a "wonky" placement. This means taking a larger wall that could normally hold a larger piece and, instead, using a smaller piece that is offset and not centered. When done right, this can feel extremely chic and surprising. Playing with scale with your artwork and design can create incredibly memorable moments.

Picture Rail

This is a traditional element found in some older homes especially with plaster walls. In order to save the texture and craftsmanship of a plaster wall, a wooden rail with a gap was installed along the upper edge. If you suspect you may have one, run your finger along the top edge of the rail to see if there is a gap for a hook. If there is, congratulations! You have the ability to hang your work from a chain and hook that gives a very elegant feel to a piece of artwork. Look for a store online that sells hardware for historic homes. You'll find picture hanging hooks as an option. Hang the upper hook from the rail, and the lower hook attaches to the wire on the backside of the artwork. A small ball of museum putty will help keep the piece level and in place without hurting the walls.

Plaster Walls

Plaster walls can be one of the most difficult surfaces to hang artwork on. Hanging artwork on these types of walls requires special care to avoid cracks and damage. If you have hung something on a plaster wall before you may have heard the telltale sign of something crumbling on the inside of the wall. Here's how to do it properly so you can hang artwork confidently.

USE THE RIGHT HARDWARE FOR THE JOB. Plaster anchors are plastic or metal anchors designed specifically to hold screws securely in plaster. Toggle bolts for heavy artwork will spread the weight behind the wall for extra support.

USE A STUD FINDER to locate wooden studs, which will offer the best support. If hanging in a hollow area use the anchors or toggle bolts.

SCREWS DO LESS DAMAGE to plaster compared to a nail and hammer if done correctly. Put a small piece of painter's tape where you'll drill to reduce the cracking. The tape will work as a support to the fine layer of plaster on top and paint. Drill slowly with a masonry or carbide-tipped bit to avoid crumbling. Then insert the anchor, if needed, and tape it gently before adding the screw.

Artwork by Shannon Coppage.
Design by Fogarty Finger.
Photo by David Mitchell / JBSA.

ANONYMOUS WAS A WOMAN
BANK
St. Martin's Press
HOLE
MARSDEN HARTLEY AND THE WEST
GEORGIA O'KEEFFE MUSEUM
YALE UNIVERSITY PRESS
Gagosian
Richard Wright

YOUR GUIDE TO

framing

Framing of an artwork can make or break your piece. It can elevate the piece, it can streamline it, or it can instantly date it. Certainly we think of framing as an aesthetic opportunity, but it also preserves the piece. A frame, at its very core, protects an artwork, which means that you want to use quality materials.

If you have ever taken apart a piece of artwork that is vintage or antique, you'll know what I am talking about. The mat often has a discoloration from light exposure and the artwork may be a different color around the edges. That discoloration can happen from light exposure but also from the acidity from the mat paper, which creates "mat burn." Mat burn is a darkening around the artwork where an artwork was exposed to poor quality materials. Several decades ago, most mats were made with a heavy wood pulp, which is chemically unstable and acidic. Fading or discoloration in the center of the piece means that most likely the artwork was framed with a non-UV filtering glazing (glass). Mat burn can be reversed in some instances but artwork fading cannot be reversed. Additionally, small bugs are very attracted to acidity, so if you've ever noticed a small bug or mite in the frame of the artwork, that's the reason!

Opposite: Artwork by James Navarro and Christina Flowers.

Framing Terms

- **BEVEL:** (1) This is the angled edge of a mat board that creates a shadow effect for dimension.
- **BRACKET:** These are plastic or metal pieces placed on the corners of the frame to keep the structure solid for reinforcements.
- **FLOAT FRAME:** This is a style of frame often used when framing canvases. It appears that the artwork is floating in the frame. Glazing is not used when a canvas is framed using a float frame.
- **GLAZING:** (2) This is the transparent cover that protects an artwork. It can be acrylic or glass but should be UV filtering.
- **HANGING HARDWARE:** (3) These are the elements used to hang an artwork on the wall. This could include D rings, wire, or a hanging claw.
- **MATTING:** (4) A paper board cut to fit around the artwork to add visual space and depth to an artwork.
- **MOUNTING:** This is the process of securing the artwork to a mounting surface to make sure the artwork does not slip.
- **PROFILE:** (5) This is the shape and design of the frame. Examples could be sleek and modern or eclectic and ornate.
- **RABBET:** This is the recessed area in the frame where the artwork and mat are placed. The rabbet holds everything in place.
- **SPACER:** A thin strip of paper placed between the artwork and the glazing to prevent them from touching.
- **STORAGE PACKET:** (6) A paper pocket on the back of the artwork to hold any specific paperwork.

FRONT OF A FRAMED PIECE

Includes a white mat with a beveled edge, glazing, and a modern, simple profile frame.

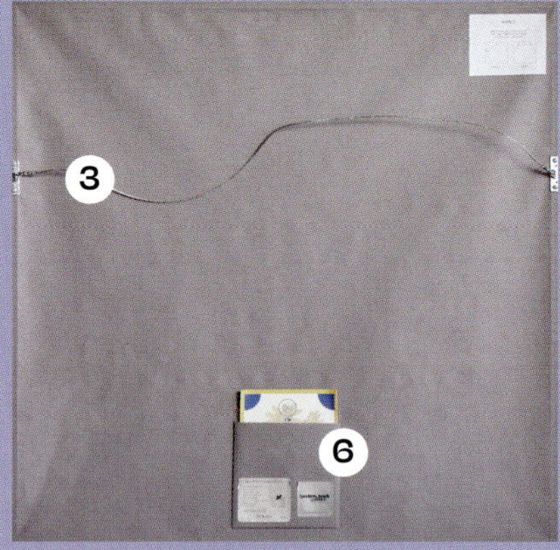

BACK OF A FRAMED PIECE

Includes hanging hardware (and internally a spacer, rabbet, and bracket) covered with a finishing paper.

OTHER FRAMING EXAMPLES

ACRYLIC BOX FRAME

FLOAT FRAME

ANTIQUE FRAME

PAINTED FRAME

HOT TIP: Ask your framer to create a storage packet on the back of the artwork to hold any specific paperwork, such as the certificate of authenticity, gallery business card, or information about the artist.

Opposite: Artwork by Shannon Coppage. *This page:* Artwork by Elisa Sheehan, Anee Shah, Rocky Reed, and Sarah Schwartz. Background artwork by Christina Flowers.

Artwork by Meghan Bustard.

Think of the frame as an extension of the artwork.

The frame's primary function is to protect an artwork, but there are many aesthetic considerations as well.

The frame should enhance, but not distract from, the piece. It's important to think about the color and style that would be most cohesive with the artwork's composition, mood, and era.

Most often I try to match the medium of the artwork, meaning a modern piece looks wonderful with a sleek "gallery black" frame. A beautiful oil painting may fit well with a more ornate or gilded frame. Of course, rules are made to be broken, and I have seen incredibly beautiful modern pieces framed in ornate frames so that the juxtaposition becomes an important part of the display.

The mat is one of the most underrated elements of the frame. You can play with proportion, color, style, and scale. Some of my favorite projects have included small pieces with a very large mat to create a much larger piece for the wall. Another option is framing a large piece with an equally large mat. Play with scale and the negative space around the piece created by the mat.

Play with trends in framing with caution. Trends in framing come and go through the years like anything else in design. In the 1990s, it was all the rage to frame anything people could get their hands on with a mauve mat and a shiny brass frame. I could have made a career out of rescuing these artworks trapped in the twentieth century—there are still so many out there in the world. In the 2020s, the trend is to play with fun non-linear shapes, with both the mats and the frame. Wavy shapes and scalloped edges have taken over, along with hand-painted mats that give an English-country feel. Quite frankly, I love both of these trends—they're right up my design alley. I think it's okay to play with trends as long as you know that someday you'll most likely want to reframe it to bring your piece into the current era. Framing does not mean, and often should not be, a one-time deal in the lifetime of the artwork.

Opposite: Background artwork by Daisy Faith.

THE MORE YOU KNOW

A new frame can not only give the piece new style-life but also releases trapped off-gassing. What is off-gassing? This occurs when materials release volatile organic compounds (VOCs) over time. These gases can come from freshly cut wood, some adhesives, non-archival mat boards, some paints, or low-quality glass. This off-gassing can turn a work on paper yellow over time. It may also make the inside of the glass look hazy or dirty. It can also weaken less-stable mediums such as watercolor or pastel.

This is why it's important to frame your artwork with quality materials that will prevent these damaging VOCs from occurring around your artwork.

Let's decide how to frame this artwork!

OPTIONS 1, 2, 3, AND 4: When you are working with a framer to decide on a frame, you'll be given a selection of framing corners so that you are able to compare the look of each. This is where you will be able to consider the aesthetics and style of a piece, material, color, matting, glazing type, artwork protection, and hanging hardware.

There is no wrong answer out of the four options. Here's what I would say if I were hanging this multi-media Bethany Mabee piece: "I'd like a simple profile frame that will go well with the modern look of the piece. The piece is 16 × 20 inches so I would like a 2.5-inch mat with a bevel. I would like museum glazing that will protect the piece from UV rays, and I would like a wire with a paper pocket on the back, please." A good rule of thumb for choosing your mat size is that the mat should be at least 1 inch larger than the width of the frame profile. If your frame is 1 inch wide, then your mat should be 2 inches, for example. Most mats are 2 to 4 inches wide.

Opposite: Artwork by Bethany Mabee.

HOW TO FRAME ON A BUDGET.

Framing can be expensive and can often add up to cost more than the artwork itself. And, unlike art where you might find a bargain in an unexpected place, the cost of framing is fairly fixed and unavoidable. There have certainly been times in my life where I did not have the budget to add a custom frame just after I purchased the artwork. I often use ready-made frames for family photos or special paper/non-artwork mementos.

My number one tip for framing on a budget is to purchase the frame and have a framer custom cut a mat for your artwork. This will give the effect of a custom frame without the price tag. Additionally, it will ensure that a high-quality mat is touching your artwork and will help prevent that dreaded mat burn.

This page: A series of vintage collected pieces including works by Nicholas Orsini and Harley Francis. Design by Andrea Brooks Interiors. Photo by Mark Jackson / CHROMA. *Opposite:* Background artwork by Bethany Mabee.

AN ARTFUL CONVERSATION WITH

DARA DESHE

FOUNDER OF THE FRAMING COMPANY SIMPLY FRAMED

Dara Deshe launched Simply Framed in 2014 to make custom framing more convenient and less expensive for consumers, artists, and art businesses. She previously worked as a merchandiser for Facebook Gifts, 20x200.com, and American Eagle. In 2023, Simply Framed merged with its manufacturer, Cali Framing Supplies. Dara is passionate about helping consumers, artists, and gallerists find the right frame to make their art shine.

LIZ: Dara, you founded the framing company Simply Framed. I am sure you have seen it all. What are some common framing mistakes you see?

DARA: Some common mistakes include choosing a mat in the wrong shade of white or framing art with a colored mat (unless it's the rare instance where the artist has very consciously selected a color of both mat and frame to enhance the art). A mat that is too small relative to the total size of the art can also work against the artwork, versus creating ample space for the art to be visually appreciated.

If the artwork has an interesting or decorative edge or signature toward the edge of the paper, then it should be floated so these details can be seen, versus covered by a mat or frame. And then finally you never want to have the glazing material (usually glass or plexiglass) touching the surface of the art—over time it can compromise the art, so that's where using a mat or a spacer are very effective.

There are countless ways to get it wrong because there's so much nuance that goes into the frame choice: the moulding's shape, finish, size, and color. The choice of glazing. The choice and size, color, material, and thickness (referred to as "ply") of the mat. How the art is mounted. I shared this because this is why we exist. It's often so easy to notice when something is wrong, but when the frame is right, the whole piece just looks right and you often don't even notice the frame. That's where the whole idea of having your art "simply framed" comes from. We take an art-first approach to framing and try to follow the same aesthetic standards used by the best galleries and museums so that ultimately the art is the focal point, not the frame!

LIZ: Of course, buying a ready-made frame from a big box retailer is a choice that is available. Can you tell me why it's really important to frame with quality materials, and can you find those materials in a ready-made frame?

DARA: It's important the art is mounted using acid-free materials, which ensure the art is not discolored with time. Ready-made frames are great for things that you think of as décor, like family photos, but over time they do not offer the same protection as high-quality acid-free materials. They also usually come with glass, which is both easily broken and does not provide any protection from the sun. At Simply Framed, we also sell our product as a "frame kit" so that if you want to have a ready-made-style frame with acid-free materials, it's possible to order one from the website with all your sizes and specifications considered.

LIZ: Do you have any general tips or rules that you think people should follow when framing their artwork?

DARA: Always choose your frame to enhance the artwork, versus match the room. When in doubt look at how art is framed in contemporary museums for reference. Great art will live and grow with you over time and will move from room to room. Your personal style is likely to evolve and it would be a shame to constantly have to re-frame an artwork because of this. We live by these words: Frame it once, frame it well.

Background artwork by Kristen Abbott.

Artwork by Taelor Fisher and Bekah Worley.

HOW TO

clean your artwork

GENERAL RULES FOR CLEANING YOUR ARTWORK

- **TEST FIRST!** I like to use a clean, dry microfiber cloth as the first attempt. If needed, you can lightly dampen the cloth to use on canvas, metal, or glass but never paper. Always test clean your artwork on a small area that is out of sightline.
- **DO NOT SPRAY A CHEMICAL NEAR YOUR ARTWORK.** Simple microfiber cloths will be your best friend.
- **WHEN IN DOUBT, GO PROFESSIONAL.** Take an artwork to your local framer or call your regional conservation center for advice if the issue is larger than dust or a mark on the frame.
- **DUST REGULARLY.** Use a dry microfiber cloth monthly to remove any dust from a canvas or frame. If you are dusting a canvas, dust in the direction of the paint strokes. Do not go against the paint.
- **CLEAN THE GLASS.** Even if the artwork is behind a glazing, you should still not spray a chemical near an artwork. Frames are not airtight, and it is possible the chemical could get between the glazing and artwork. Instead, use a mixture of water and vinegar in a spray bottle. Spray your cloth first and then rub the solution onto the glazing.
- **ACCIDENTS HAPPEN** and if for some reason a mark happens near your painting, you can test clean the mark with a barely damp microfiber cloth, rubbing gently. Often this helps. If not, call a professional.
- **FOR TEXTILES, YOU MAY USE A VACUUM.** If the textile is not fragile, you may use a low-setting vacuum. I find that handheld vacuums are better because they do not have the power and strength of a traditional floor vacuum.

AN ARTFUL CONVERSATION WITH

JEN MUNCH

OWNER OF JEN MUNCH ART CONSERVATION

Jen Munch is an art conservator and the owner of Jen Munch Art Conservation, a Brooklyn-based business specializing in the care of modern and contemporary paintings for collectors, museums, galleries, artists, and their estates. Jen is a professional associate of the American Institute for Conservation and served as the Chair of AIC's Contemporary Art Network for 2022–24.

LIZ: What are a few tips you wish every art owner would follow?

JEN: You can and should insure your art. Insurance comes in handy if your art is accidentally damaged and needs to be treated by a conservator. I have treated art damaged by various types of flooding and fire, as well as damage incurred during shipping. Speak with your insurance agent about how to insure your art for its full value. Otherwise, any payout may be capped at a low amount.

For art that will hang on a wall using hooks or screws, always secure your artworks onto two hangers, not just one. Using two hangers versus one means that there's an extra safeguard in case one hanger malfunctions. It's an inexpensive way to prevent art from falling off the wall. For most uses, I recommend the type of wall hooks called "floreats," which are a style used in museums. However, if you're in an earthquake-prone area or live right above a subway, you should opt for earthquake picture hangers.

LIZ: What do you think are the most preventable mistakes with artwork?

JEN: You can prevent a lot of issues by simply keeping your art in locations with the most stable climate. Big swings in humidity and temperature wreak havoc and cause issues, especially for works on paper and for paintings. Bathrooms are one of the worst locations for hanging art, for that reason. I also see condition issues caused by hanging art in areas where people cook or eat. If you really want art in a bathroom, for instance, go for something that is easily replaceable and has low sentimental value. If you decide to place art someplace where someone could splash food or liquids onto it, take measures to help prevent damage by having the art protected by a frame with glazing, and select a location that is as far out of harm's way as possible. You probably already know that sunlight can fade some pigments and dyes, so it's also a good idea to avoid hanging paintings, textiles, or works on paper in direct sunlight. The good news is that "inorganic" materials (those made of stone or metal) are often fine in direct sunlight. Just a note about storage: You can generally store art safely in a closet in your living space, but attics and basements are not ideal choices because they have climate swings that can lead to mold growth and other issues.

Another of the most preventable mistakes occurs when owners clean art themselves, or have housekeepers clean the art. Art is made of different materials than other goods in your home or office. Unlike your dishware or flooring, most art is not designed to be easy to clean. Broadly speaking, artworks in good condition can be gently dusted with a soft brush after thoroughly examining the work and making sure it's safe to do so. Other than that, always leave art cleaning to a professional conservator. Conservators frequently see artworks damaged by well-intentioned home cleaning attempts.

Anytime art is moved there's a risk of damaging it. You can lower that risk by planning your path before carrying art. Also, be sure to hold two-dimensional works by any two edges, versus just holding it along the top edge, to prevent putting too much strain on one area.

LIZ: What can be done once damage has happened? For example, a small tear in a canvas?

JEN: Once damage has happened, contact a professional conservator. If you're in the United States, our national professional association, the American Institute for Conservation, has a free online tool called "Find a Conservator" that will help you find a qualified professional near you. You can also contact a local museum or historical society to ask who they recommend.

Background artwork by Jennifer Allevato.

LET THERE

be light!

The right lighting can really enhance your artwork, because if you can't see the artwork, you can't enjoy it! Lighting your artwork incorrectly or too harshly can detract from or harm the piece, so it pays to get it right. Here are some good rules of thumb for lighting your artwork.

- **LED LIGHTS ARE THE WAY TO GO.** LEDs are the go-to for professionals because they have a longer lifespan, produce less heat, and come in a variety of color temperatures.
- **LOOK FOR LIGHTS** between 2700K and 3000K. This color temperature will help display the artwork beautifully, while being less harsh.
- **REPEAT AFTER ME:** 45-degree angle. A 45-degree angle is going to cast a gorgeous light over the piece and not create shadows. Shadows are the number one visual issue I see happening. They make the artwork look darker and, oftentimes, off-center. A 45-degree angle will also help reduce glare if there is glazing on the artwork.
- **AVOID DIRECT SUNLIGHT.** If LED lights are your friend then sunlight is your enemy. Those UV rays can fade artwork, which we learned earlier is irreversible. Even if you have a UV-filtering glazing, direct sunlight will damage artwork.
- **A PICTURE LIGHT** is a horizontal, usually wall-mounted light that illuminates a piece of artwork. Occasionally, they are mounted directly to an artwork's frame as an alternative. Picture lights should be 6 to 7 inches above an artwork. Position the light directly in the center of the piece so that the light can wash over the entire piece. Choose a picture light that is about half the entire length of the artwork. Then tilt the light down so that it is between a 35- and 45- degree angle.

Opposite: Artwork by Julie Blackmon. Design by Elsie Larson. Photo by Katie Day.

Artwork by Bethany Mabee. Design by Jamie Ivey, Ivey Design Group. Photo by Ansel Olson.

HOW TO

store your artwork

There will be times throughout your collecting journey when you may need to store artwork for a period of time. No matter the length of time, you'll want to store your artwork in a clean, dry, and temperature-controlled location. Unfortunately, major damage can occur from humidity and large swings in temperature will affect any piece of artwork. Wood and paper are especially susceptible to these issues.

FOR A SHORT PERIOD OF TIME (LESS THAN SIX MONTHS). The number one rule of artwork storing is this: front to front, back to back. If you are ever in a situation where you are stacking artwork, make sure that the fronts of frames are toward each other and the backs of frames are toward each other. Often the backs of artwork have hardware that can scratch and damage a frame or canvas. Even when an artwork is wrapped in a packing blanket, paper, or bubble wrap you will want to follow this rule. Artwork hardware easily pokes through many materials and damage can occur. If you are storing artwork for a short period of time (one month or less), you can lay a piece of acid-free board onto the ground and a piece of board in between each artwork.

FOR A LONG PERIOD OF TIME (MORE THAN SIX MONTHS). If you need to store artwork for a longer period of time, I recommend wrapping each artwork using clean, high-quality materials. Bubble wrap and packing blankets are both options to wrap a piece of artwork in once it has been protected by an acid-free paper or material. Do not use packing tape to seal and secure the artwork. Often this type of tape needs to be cut to open the piece again and we want to avoid sharp objects near your artwork. Painting tape will secure the material and is easily removable.

You will want to make sure that the area has proper ventilation so that no mold can grow on or near your artwork. Finally, check on your artwork throughout the storage process to confirm that the storage situation has not changed without you being aware.

Artwork by Elsie Larson and Anee Shah.
Design by Massop House.

This page: Artwork by Hayley Sheldon. *Opposite:* Background artwork by Christina Flowers.

CHAPTER

THINK Outside THE BOX

LOOKING
BEYOND STYLING
ART THE
OLD-FASHIONED
WAY

EIGHT

This is where I tell you to forget all the rules that I just taught you in chapter seven. Truly though, once you become a master in hanging a piece of artwork and understand the rules, then you can feel free to break them with confidence. Think beyond just hanging a single piece of artwork in the center of the wall. This is where you can channel your creativity and inner artist for your arrangements. I am looking for that flow around corners, artwork above doorways or on windows. Your artwork can become the driving force of the design by stepping outside the traditional ways to hang art.

These are some of my favorite ways to incorporate artwork into your home.

This page: Background artwork by Kristen Abbott. *Opposite:* Artwork by Michael Peter Cain and Kit Porter.

A VOS CRAYONS!

MIX YOUR ARTWORK WITH functional ITEMS

The fact is that a home, no matter how lovely or how diligent the homeowners are, is not a pristine gallery. This means we have to contend with the functional necessity of living in a home.

HOW: Search for a variety of artwork styles that have cohesive elements and even empty frames.

WHY IT WORKS: The design and artwork shows how you can play with the architecture of home and still hang a large piece when the room is surrounded by windows. Artwork can always work with functional and necessary elements of a room like windows or even thermostats and television sets. Art can creatively disguise a view you may not want to regularly see, or by including functional items, art can distract from utilitarian items.

Opposite: Artwork is a framed vintage Hermès scarf. Design by Lisa Gilmore Design. Photo by Amy Lamb.

INCLUDE YOUR

kids and pets!

A wonderful client of ours has created the ultimate gallery wall in her home. She has purchased artwork over time that she finds joyful and when she planned the ultimate gallery wall, she knew she wanted to include her pets in the wall. The wooden shelving waves are for her cats to climb and rest among the beautiful pieces she has collected, becoming a piece of artwork themselves.

HOW: Use the skills you have learned to gather artwork for a gallery wall while adding in décor such as cat ledges or a display for toys for the children in your life.

WHY IT WORKS: By incorporating the floating cat beds, the homeowner has added a visual element that keeps the viewer's eye traveling while also making her pets a part of the art. While, perhaps, not right for every person's pets, it's an out-of-the-box moment worth sharing to get your creativity flowing.

Opposite: Background artwork by Kevin Brent Morris.

DON'T WAIT!

I have lost count of the number of times someone has come into my gallery and said, "I would love to purchase an artwork for my home, it would make me so happy, but—I have little kids at home . . . I have a rental . . . I have pets." Insert any reason that is very valid in their minds but in reality can be worked around. My plea for you: Don't wait for your life to look a certain way before you create a home that you love. At first, you may be working on a thrift store budget. I've been there (and still enjoy the hunt). At first, you may be looking all over Facebook Marketplace instead of heading to an artist or gallery for an original piece of artwork. That's okay! Great style can happen at any budget level. It may take more time and patience to find what you are looking for, but I can tell you from firsthand experience, I have lived on many different budget levels in my adult life as I was building my business. I have taken my father along to some fairly sketchy places to pick up the score of a century (or so I felt passionately at the time). Don't wait until your kids are older to live among beautiful things. Kids will adapt and learn to live respectfully with the things around them. My children have lived every day of their life around original artwork. We live with a very large dog and two mischievous cats. Ultimately, I want to lead a beautiful life, and for me, that includes creating a beautiful (not necessarily expensive) home.

Morris

Artwork by Bekah Worley, Paige Barnes Dorsey, Carrie Gillen, Elisa Sheehan, Ron Giusti, Jessi Raulet, Kristi Kohut, Christi Meril, Melissa Ellis, Alex Hunt, and Laurie Lindqvist. Photo by Amy Long Photos.

Artwork by Christina Flowers, Monica Ajenjo, and Katie Craig.

COUNT YOUR windows AS WALL SPACE TOO

Whether you are blocking a view, creating privacy, or just need a little more wall space, consider hanging artwork over a window frame.

HOW: This is an image from my own home where I put the nail in the wood above the window and included a large white grosgrain ribbon to disguise the nail and wire that peeks up above the artwork.

WHY IT WORKS: The door to the porch perfectly frames the painting by artist Lola Donoghue. I love to include artwork near windows using blues and greens in the color palette to bring the outdoor landscape to life inside.

WHILE WE ARE TALKING WINDOWS, LET'S HANG ARTWORK ABOVE THEM (OR BELOW).

The space above and below windows is often ignored real estate when hanging artwork. By centering artwork in that space, you create an architectural moment where the frame acts like wainscoting or a chair rail.

HOW: Find an artwork that is not horizontally longer than the window frame, so that you can center the piece above the window.

WHY IT WORKS: It's an unexpected element on wall space that is often unused.

Opposite: Artwork by Lola Donoghue.

Your shelving

IS ALSO A GREAT OPPORTUNITY

In a library space, where the books themselves can be artwork, using the wood supports as a place to hang artwork helps break up the pattern and complement the paint color on the shelves.

HOW: My shelves are not custom and so I felt comfortable putting a nail directly into the wood support. If you do not, the 3M hooks used for holiday directions work well for artwork up to fifteen pounds.

WHY IT WORKS: The books act as a repeating pattern, almost like wallpaper, and are a wide, flat, wall-like surface. The artwork adds additional color and texture.

Artwork by Roma Osowo.

LAYER YOUR

mirror with art

Our client moved into a grand home that included a large mirrored accent wall. The mirror felt dated when left alone so we decided to add a personal piece of artwork gifted by a family member into the center of the mirror. It took this 1980s wall from dated to modern almost instantly.

HOW: We used a heavy-duty double-sided table to attach the artwork to the mirrored wall. I stuck the tape directly to the backside of the frame and created a border on all four sides to ensure maximum hold.

WHY IT WORKS: This kind of design element has the ability to skew dated but the large velvet curtains and antique print bring it to a more traditional style that feels classic.

Layering your artwork with a mirror allows any display to be temporary. This is also a style that feels much more casual and can be a wonderful contrast to more formal designs.

HOW: Use the mirror as your first central layer. Then layer smaller artworks on the edges so that the mirror can peek through and reflect portions of the room around you to create the illusion of a larger space. Layering the artwork with sculptures and vintage finds will continue to round out the design. Remember the rule of thirds to divide objects throughout the space.

WHY IT WORKS: This fits a lot of different interior design styles and gives you the freedom to switch things up if you're someone who gets bored easily with your style.

Opposite: Artwork by Kevin Brent Morris and a vintage piece. Background artwork by Theodora Miller.

HIDE YOUR

television set

WITH A WORK OF ART

Televisions are the bane of every designer's existence, I think. They provide a dark void in an otherwise beautiful space, and they take up valuable real estate in a room. Now, we all understand that televisions are here to stay, and we need to find ways to incorporate them in fun ways: include the television in a gallery wall like from chapter six or cover the TV entirely with an artwork for the times it's not on.

HOW: There's two ways I would recommend using artwork to cover your television set. The first would be with a rope and pulley system if you have the ceiling height. By attaching pulleys to your ceiling, you will have leverage to pull up the artwork to watch your favorite reality show or release it down to hide the television.

The second way is by creating a panel system of artwork to cover the television using bi-fold doors, which collapse and swing out of the way. This system works for areas that do not have the ceiling height or are more compact.

WHY IT WORKS: This adds versatility and flexibility to your space. We all want options and more potential locations for artwork, right? As formal and informal spaces are merging more and more in homes, this offers options depending on how you are currently using the space.

WATERPROOF YOUR ARTWORK TO

hang it outside

I'd like to start this idea with a caveat. I have done this process in my own home, but I used an inexpensive piece that I thrifted. This is not for valuable works because depending on your climate, the artwork will likely still deteriorate over time. I live in a climate with all four seasons, high highs and low lows in temperature, and my piece lasted for five years before I replaced it.

HOW: There is a specific product that I recommend: Scotchguard Outdoor Waterproof Seal spray. I found an artwork at my local thrift shop for $5. It was large and made of canvas with a wood frame.

I suggest using a canvas piece—nothing where moisture can be trapped, such as an artwork with a glass protecting it. Frames are not airtight. Moisture will get in but will have a tougher time releasing.

WHY IT WORKS: Murals are a lovely option for outdoor artwork but they require a commitment by the homeowner. If you'd like to test out the theory that artwork would look beautiful outside your home, near your patio, or even along a fence line, try this option first.

WRAP YOUR GALLERY WALL

around a corner

This technique takes your gallery wall skills from chapter six to the next level, making it known that you are a true art installation expert.

HOW: You'll need a room where two walls conjoin and make a 90-degree angle. This is easier said than done with windows and door openings getting in the way. BUT if you have the perfect setup, this is a fun way to play with the typical idea of a gallery wall.

WHY IT WORKS: This works wonderfully if there are many pieces that you would like to include in a gallery wall without making the design seem too cluttered. It also adds some major design interest in an otherwise uninteresting corner by drawing your eye from one end to the other. Visually, the mural underneath the artwork—by artist Racheal Jackson in the home of designer Andrea Brooks—connects the gallery wall and continues your eye throughout the large wall space.

Opposite: Artwork by Mione Plant, Mike Sajnoski, and Ashley Longshore. Wall mural by Racheal Jackson. Design by Andrea Brooks Interiors. Photo by Mark Jackson / CHROMA.

DISPLAY ART ON

easels

When you think of art on easels, you most likely think of the artist actively creating a work in progress. I, however, also think that art can be beautifully displayed on easels in your home.

HOW: Small easels have become an item I must take home when I am thrifting. They are perfect for when you have run out of wall space or want to create a layered look, like in the photo opposite. Other ideas include using large standing easels as partitions in a room or to block an unpleasant view. It also elevates the look by putting an emphasis on the piece that draws viewers in. I talked about this earlier, specifically for renters, but it applies to everyone!

WHY IT WORKS: This is an easy-execution, high-on-style type of art display. It makes it simple to change and replace artwork through the seasons and requires no holes in your walls. I look for both tabletop and floor easels when I am thrifting. Extra bonus points if there is a light attached as well.

Opposite: Artwork by Hillary Howorth and a vintage piece.

LEAN ART ON

picture ledges

While we are talking about low-commitment ways to display art, let's talk about the art of leaning art. This is first and foremost a way for your artwork collection to feel a little less formal. It feels casual and lived in. This is the equivalent of those very chic women you know who just "throw things on" and look perfect. Much thought has gone into it, but it feels effortless.

HOW: The easy answer would be to just layer and lean the artwork, but it's more nuanced than that. Goals for this will be to make sure that enough of the art is visible, none of the art is putting pressure on another piece of art where it would leave a mark, and that the design ratios work. Odd numbers usually work best. You'll want to vary the size of the pieces and styles so that your eye moves throughout the arrangement and does not create any straight lines across.

WHY IT WORKS: Just as the easel is a simple, noncommittal way to display artwork, so is leaning artwork on a picture ledge or above a fireplace. I also think this is a lovely way to layer artwork and family photos to create a highly personalized arrangement that can change easily.

Opposite: Artwork by Keren Fraser and Susannah Carson, paired with vintage pieces. Background artwork by Kristen Abbott.

NO VIP PASS NEEDED

ART IS FOR EVERYONE

While writing this book, I had the opportunity to travel to Mexico City and visit Frida Kahlo's home and museum, Casa Azul. Going to her home felt like an art world pilgrimage. After reading so many books and essays and even creating a podcast episode about her and her work, seeing the home she created—full of art, of course—filled in a missing piece to understanding Frida. You see where she created art in her studio and her bedroom but also that her house itself was a piece of art. Murals are hand painted on walls, rich color is everywhere, and art is installed in the most beautiful and creative ways. There was a sign in the museum that I think of often now. One section read, "These walls preserve what cannot be found elsewhere. Frida's belongings speak of her everyday life and her process as an artist in constant transformation. The house is not merely about decorating walls, but rather a declaration of principles." *Mic. Drop.*

Frida understood that one's home can be, and arguably should be, a representation of loves, interests, and ideologies. It can show the way someone sees the world. The sign also read, "Day by day, she turns her house into an extension of herself." Each sign spoke of Frida in the present. Although she died in 1954, this felt right because she felt alive in her home. It remains a great testament to her life and creativity.

This does not happen all at once. It happens through your many choices, big and small, that slowly, piece by piece, create a design that represents you and your family. Slow design is a theory that involves thoughtful consideration and fine tuning. It also focuses on the well-being of people in that home or space. It argues against going to a store and purchasing an entire room in one go. It means buying the

Artwork by Neicy Frey.
Design by Massop House.

Artwork by Jessi Raulet, Karin Olah, Angie Barker, Betsy Enzensberger, Logan Ledford, Makiko Harris, Anee Shah, and Jose Romussi.

"right" piece of furniture and the "right" piece of art versus buying something right away for the convenience of the now-now-now. This takes patience, of course, but slowly you can build a space where you love every single thing.

The journal *Slow Living London* defines the six principles of slow design as reveal, expand, reflect, engage, participate, and evolve. Since reading them, I have kept each one in the back of my mind while I am designing my home and my clients' spaces. I believe each principle can be interpreted and applied differently but I love how each encourages a thoughtfulness that is sometimes eschewed in design for immediate results. Applying these principles to buying artwork specifically means learning how to find the pieces that bring you joy. Finding the patience to discover the artwork that you want to spend the rest of your life living next to, and sometimes living with a blank wall until you find what's right.

I have always believed that each artwork is created for a specific person to find and that masterpieces, specifically those few pieces that can be called so, are made for the world. One of the exciting things for me as a gallery owner is that I believe my role is connecting each artwork with the person it was created for. Yes, it's all a bit woo-woo, but when I see someone connecting with an artwork that they truly love it feels magical. My wish for everyone reading this book is that you feel, at some point—or hopefully many times—that magic for yourself. You feel it the moment you connect with a piece that was meant to find you.

The art market in 2024 was estimated to reach almost $10 billion. While those are astronomical numbers, I hope you won't be discouraged. That figure includes artwork selling for millions of dollars at the auction houses all the way down to artwork being sold for $100 at a local art fair. It is a vast and wide-ranging market that has a way for everyone to enter. If you continue to explore and educate yourself about artwork, you will find your place and where you belong. Of this, I am certain. The art world is meant for everyone and that means you.

And once you find your place and the artwork you love and the artists that inspire you, I think you may become addicted. There is a rush in finding that magic, seeing the beauty and simultaneously supporting an artist and a small business. I think often of a study that I read several years ago. In it the participants overwhelmingly indicated that they valued art in their communities. At the same time, they also indicated that they did not value artists. Who did they think was creating the art they valued? What the participants did not seem to understand is that artists are a necessary and integral part of society. That creative expression is necessary to inspire, bring beauty, and hold a mirror up to our communities. By buying artwork from a gallery or artist, by supporting an artist, you are using your dollars to create the type of world you want to live in. Enabling artists to create and live is one of the things I am most proud of in my career.

As my writing is coming to an end, I hope that your journey into the art world is just beginning. You will find artwork that you love . . . and artwork that you don't. You will find artwork you can afford . . . and artwork you can't. You will meet people in the art world you adore . . . and those you don't. It all matters, though, so keep going until you find your place. Over time, you will slowly and deliberately build a collection that speaks to you. You'll create a home full of art that you love, and just like Frida, you'll make a home that is an extension of you.

Artwork by Jennifer Allevato.

ADDITIONAL RESOURCES: READING LIST

I am a voracious reader and one of my love languages is recommending books. If you'd love to read more about art and the art world, these are some of my favorite books.

***What Are You Looking At?* by Will Gompertz**
Gompertz takes you through each major art movement of the last 150 years. The book shows how each movement built off prior work and the connective tissue between artists and styles.

***How Art Can Change Your Life* by Susie Hodge**
Hodge shares some of the most famous works of art in art history and groups them by how they can make you feel or help you. These groups include "relieving stress" or "gaining inspiration."

***The Story of Art Without Men* by Katy Hessel**
Hessel discusses more than 300 works of art by women artists, sharing a new art history that showcases often untold stories. She also puts a spotlight on contemporary women artists who are working today.

***Ninth Street Women* by Mary Gabriel**
Gabriel weaves the stories of five women artists who dared to enter the male-dominated field of abstract painting during the twentieth century. Their tales are empowering, sometimes tragic and frustrating, but all intriguing.

***Art: The Definitive Visual Guide* by Andrew Graham Dixon**
A beautiful coffee table book that will serve as an encyclopedic reference from some of the most incredible pieces that span the entirety of art history.

***Art Is Life: Icons and Iconoclasts, Visionaries and Vigilantes, and Flashes of Hope in the Night* by Jerry Saltz**
Saltz is a Pulitzer Prize–winning art critic and writer and this book brings together essays about some of the most important artists working today. I also highly recommend his book *How to be an Artist*, which has nuggets of wisdom that can be applied to anyone's life.

***Get the Picture: A Mind-Bending Journey Among the Inspired Artists and Obsessive Art Fiends Who Taught Me How to See* by Bianca Bosker**
I'll admit that at times Bosker's book was triggering for me because she writes of an elite art world that often looks down at beginning collectors. However, she is a great writer and tells interesting stories about becoming involved with the blue-chip art world.

***Seven Days in the Art World* by Sarah Thornton**
Thornton spends a day with seven different art world representatives. She details their version of the art world and how their roles fit into the larger ecosystem.

***The $12 Million Stuffed Shark: The Curious Economics of Contemporary Art* by Don Thompson**
Thompson explores the money and economics behind the art world and some of those larger-than-life prices that make the headlines.

ADDITIONAL RESOURCES: TRAVEL LIST

Want to see more art? The following list is my travel bucket list for art world pilgrimages. I have had the opportunity to see some of these incredible places and institutions with my own eyes and some are still just a dream. Here are my top art travel recommendations.

The Americas

NEW YORK, NY

What to see: The Metropolitan Museum of Art, the Museum of Modern Art, Whitney Museum of American Art, the Frick Collection, and the Guggenheim

Why? New York has it all and you can see so much incredible art in a short period of time. I have listed museums above, but of course, some of the biggest galleries in the world are also in Chelsea and SoHo.

MEXICO CITY, MEXICO

What to see: Frida Kahlo Museum, Museo Tamayo, and Museo del Palacio de Bellas Artes

Why? The mix of art styles and vibrancy of the city make this a must-travel destination for art lovers.

Honorable Mentions: In the United States, I'd also add the J. Paul Getty Museum in Los Angeles, and a visit to Marfa, TX, an art-obsessed city that gained prominence thanks to Donald Judd and the Chinati Foundation.

Europe

PARIS, FRANCE

What to see: Louvre Museum, Musée d'Orsay, Centre Pompidou, Musée De l'Orangerie

Why? Paris is *the* city in art history and it remains home to some of the most incredible collections in the world.

A lovely day trip from Paris is to take a train to Giverny to see Claude Monet's home and gardens. If you opt for a guided tour, you can often include Versailles.

Additionally, a highlight of my art world life was traveling to the Périgord region in southern France to see the cave paintings created by people 20,000 to 40,000 years ago. Art connects us through lifetimes.

FLORENCE, ITALY

What to see: Uffizi Gallery, Galleria dell'Accademia, and Pitti Palace

Why? Florence is the birthplace of the Renaissance. It has been preserved in such beautiful ways that each street feels like you are discovering a new museum.

VENICE, ITALY

What to see: Peggy Guggenheim Collection, Accademia Gallery Museum, and, if you are traveling during an event year, the Venice Biennale

Why? The Biennale is one of the top contemporary events for the art world. Each participating country takes over a pavilion in the city to share some of the top working artists their country has to offer.

BERLIN, GERMANY

What to see: Museum Island, Berlinische Galerie, and East Side Gallery

Why? Berlin has become known as a center for experimental and avant-garde art. It also boasts one of the top street art scenes in the world.

MADRID, SPAIN

What to see: Prado Museum, Museo Nacional Thyssen-Bornemisza, and Reina Sofía

Why? Their collections are filled with Spanish masters like Picasso, Goya, and Velázquez. Enjoy the capital of flamenco while walking through the park-lined streets and enjoying a bite at the world's oldest restaurant.

LONDON, ENGLAND

What to see: Tate Modern, Victoria and Albert Museum, the National Gallery, and British Museum

Why? London has such a rich history and an enviable amount of museums that are free to the public, making culture accessible to the masses.

Asia

TOKYO, JAPAN

What to see: Mori Art Museum, National Museum of Modern Art, TeamLab Planets

Why? You'll be able to see art that spans thousands of years from 10,000 BCE to some of the most futuristic digital art happening today. Japan has deep-rooted traditional aesthetics while blending itself with contemporary art.

Honorable mention: Naoshima, a tiny island located in the Seto Inland Sea, is Japan's "art island." It's home to sculptures and installations and modern museums and galleries, all created in the last few decades due in large part to an art-loving Japanese businessman's vision.

ADDITIONAL LOCATIONS TO HAVE ON YOUR RADAR:

Cape Town, South Africa, has a burgeoning art scene with beautiful landscapes of mountains and coastline as a backdrop.

Beijing and Shanghai, China, are significant cities for the global contemporary art scene. Check out their thriving galleries and art districts, which blend both a long history (Cai Lun is credited with inventing *paper* in China in 105 CE, for goodness sake) and an avant-garde art scene.

Miami, Florida, is taken over by the art world every year in early December. Art Basel Miami Beach is one of the biggest and most prestigious art fairs in the United States. It is an extension of the Art Basel fair system that was originally founded in Basel, Switzerland, in 1970 and now has iterations in Miami Beach, Hong Kong, and Paris.

ACKNOWLEDGMENTS

Writing this book has been a dream come true from start to finish. From being connected to an incredible agent, to the world's most amazing editor landing in my DM's at the exact right time, to seeing the design for the first time, this process has been filled with big and small moments of joy. This has been a goal and a dream of mine for almost a decade and writing this acknowledgments page feels a bit like my shot to give an awards speech and thank everyone who has helped along the way.

Thank you to the wonderfully talented people at Simon Element including Samantha Weiner, Maria Espinosa, Gina Navarolli, and Jen Wang. You all made this process so much fun. Sam, we've used the term "kismet" since day one on this book. Thank you for believing in it. Kirsten Neuhaus, you were my voice of reason and experience throughout this process. Thank you for making this dream a reality.

Thank you to all the people who let us use their artwork, their designs, and their homes. I know how personal it is to have your space or artwork shared with the world and it means so much that you would trust me with that honor. An extra thank you to the Syversons, Cutlers, Massops, Ehrlichs, Wagners, Hamms, and my parents for letting us take over your space. Thank you to Adam Albright for being the main photographer for the book. I am thankful for your expertise and kindness for each shoot.

Thank you to my team at the gallery—Tina, Lily, Sara, Hannah, and Lauren—thank you for working on this project alongside me and for picking up the slack when I would have to remove myself from the gallery to write. Tina, thank you for being at my side through this whole crazy journey. I am so lucky. This book was such a labor of love and would not have been possible without you. I love what we do and relish doing it with all of you. To our artists, you make my world go round. Thank you for creating such beauty every day. To our clients, I truly believe you are the best clients in the entire world. Your generosity, support, and love of art make all the difference. To the designers who allowed us to share their beautiful work with the world, thank you. A special shoutout to Andrea Brooks, who created the cover photo room. Your support and kindness is so appreciated.

Thank you to my family and friends for believing in me and this book when it was nothing more than a dream. I am so lucky to have the world's best parents who have believed in me unconditionally since the day I was born. Believing in this project was no different. I just feel thankful I have the opportunity to thank you in a published(!!!) book. To Kate, you're my cheerleader and bestie. Thanks for helping with my outfits and buying so much art. You're the best. To Alex, thank you for all the support and love, it was felt all the way from Colorado. Speaking of thankful, I have the world's greatest friends. My love for all of you knows no limits. To N,S,K—What's what is what, my friends.

To Nick, Rocky, and Effie, you three are my whole world. R and E, I am proud of this book but it pales in comparison to how proud I am of you and always will be. You two are the best thing I have ever made. Watching you grow into your own people is the joy of a lifetime. N, you're it for me, kid. Thank you for being my best friend and every other good thing. I always say I married my favorite writer, so you're next.

Vintage artwork.

Art by Michelle Armas.
Design and photo by Sherry Petersik, Young House Love.

INDEX

Note: Page references in italics refer to illustrations.

Art by Logan Ledford and Aly Ytterberg.

Artwork by AK Hardeman. Photo by Adam Albright.

ABOUT THE AUTHOR

Liz Lidgett is an art adviser, writer, and gallery owner. As founder of Liz Lidgett Gallery + Design, she works with clients to find the perfect piece of art for their style, space, and budget. Liz has also been a contributor to many national publications, such as *Better Homes and Gardens*, *Martha Stewart Living*, and more. She lives in Des Moines, Iowa, with her husband and children and their ever-expanding art collection. Visit LizLidgett.com for more information.